AF567147

The Gospel of Luke

The Gospel of Luke

James C. Miller

Copyright 2019 by James C. Miller

All rights reserved. No part of this publication may be reproduced, stored in a retrieval system, or transmitted, in any form or by any means—electronic, mechanical, photocopying, recording, or otherwise—without prior written permission, except for brief quotations in critical reviews or articles.

Scripture quotations are taken from the Holy Bible, New International Version®, NIV® Copyright © 1973, 1978, 1984, 2011 by Biblica, Inc.™ Used by permission of Zondervan. All rights reserved worldwide. www.zondervan.com The "NIV" and "New International Version" are trademarks registered in the United States Patent and Trademark Office by Biblica, Inc.™ All rights reserved worldwide.

Scripture quotations marked ESV are from the ESV® Bible (The Holy Bible, English Standard Version®), copyright © 2001 by Crossway, a publishing ministry of Good News Publishers. Used by permission. All rights reserved.

Scripture quotations marked NRSV are taken from New Revised Standard Version Bible, copyright © 1989 National Council of the Churches of Christ in the United States of America. Used by permission. All rights reserved.

Scripture quotations marked TNIV are taken from the HOLY BIBLE, TODAY'S NEW INTERNATIONAL VERSION®. Copyright © 2001, 2005 by Biblica®. Used by permission of Biblica®. All rights reserved worldwide.

Scripture quotations marked KJV are taken from the Holy Bible, King James Version, Cambridge, 1796.

Printed in the United States of America

Cover design by Strange Last Name
Page design by PerfecType, Nashville, Tennessee

Miller, James C., 1956-
The Gospel of Luke / James C. Miller. – Franklin, Tennessee : Seedbed Publishing, ©2019.

pages ; cm. + 1 videodisc – (OneBook. Daily-weekly)

ISBN 9781628246810 (paperback)
ISBN 9781628246858 (DVD)
ISBN 9781628246827 (Mobi)
ISBN 9781628246834 (ePub)
ISBN 9781628246841 (uPDF)

1. Bible. Luke -- Textbooks. 2. Bible. Luke -- Study and teaching.
3. Bible. Luke -- Commentaries. I. Title. II. Series.

BS2596.M54 2019 226.4/0071 2019944159

SEEDBED PUBLISHING
Franklin, Tennessee
seedbed.com

CONTENTS

Week Four

Week Five

Week Six

Week Seven

Week Eight

WELCOME TO ONEBOOK DAILY-WEEKLY

John Wesley, in a letter to one of his leaders, penned the following:

> O begin! Fix some part of every day for private exercises. You may acquire the taste which you have not: what is tedious at first, will afterwards be pleasant. Whether you like it or not, read and pray daily. It is for your life; there is no other way; else you will be a trifler all your days. . . . Do justice to your own soul; give it time and means to grow. Do not starve yourself any longer. Take up your cross and be a Christian altogether.

Rarely are our lives most shaped by our biggest ambitions and highest aspirations. Rather, our lives are most shaped, for better or for worse, by those small things we do every single day.

At Seedbed, our biggest ambition and highest aspiration is to resource the followers of Jesus to become lovers and doers of the Word of God every single day, to become people of One Book.

To that end, we have created the OneBook Daily-Weekly. First, it's important to understand what this is not: warm, fuzzy, sentimental devotions. If you engage the Daily-Weekly for any length of time, you will learn the Word of God. You will grow profoundly in your love for God, and you will become a passionate lover of people.

How Does the Daily-Weekly Work?

Daily. As the name implies, every day invites a short but substantive engagement with the Bible. Five days a week you will read a passage of Scripture followed by a short segment of teaching and closing with questions for refection and self-examination. On the sixth day, you will review and reflect on the previous five days.

Weekly. Each week, on the seventh day, find a way to gather with at least one other person doing the study. Pursue the weekly guidance for gathering. Share learning, insight, encouragement, and most important, how the Holy Spirit is working in your lives.

That's it. Depending on the length of the study, when the eight or twelve weeks are done, we will be ready with the next study. On an ongoing basis, we will release new editions of the Daily-Weekly. Over time, those who pursue this course of learning will develop a rich library of Bible learning resources for the long haul.

OneBook Daily-Weekly will develop eight- and twelve-week studies that cover the entire Old and New Testaments. Seedbed will publish new studies regularly so that an ongoing supply of group lessons will be available. All titles will remain accessible, which means they can be used in any order that fits your needs or the needs of your group.

If you are looking for a substantive study to learn Scripture through a steadfast method, look no further.

WEEK ONE

Jesus the King

ONE

Luke 1:1–4

Luke 1:1–4 *Many have undertaken to draw up an account of the things that have been fulfilled among us, [2]just as they were handed down to us by those who from the first were eyewitnesses and servants of the word. [3]With this in mind, since I myself have carefully investigated everything from the beginning, I too decided to write an orderly account for you, most excellent Theophilus, [4]so that you may know the certainty of the things you have been taught.*

Key Observation. God's Word, given to us through Luke, can be fully trusted.

Understanding the Word. Luke 1–2 contain some of the most beloved stories about Jesus. Christians recite portions of these chapters yearly in song, in liturgy, and in Christmas plays manned by children dressed up to look like Mary and Joseph, shepherds and sheep. For many of us, the words of Linus recited from Luke 2 echo in our head from years of watching *A Charlie Brown Christmas*: "For unto you is born this day in the city of David a Saviour, which is Christ the Lord" (2:11 KJV).

But these chapters do far more than tell us delightful stories of the angel Gabriel and the baby Jesus. Through the events focused on the birth of John the Baptist and Jesus, Luke introduces us to the key themes that provide clues to all that follows.

In one sense, Luke looks backward to identify these themes, anchoring the birth of these two children within the long story of Israel. Through the words of Gabriel to Zechariah (1:13–17) and to Mary (1:28–37) we learn that their sons would occupy key roles in God's salvation promised long ago through

Israel's prophets. But Luke also looks forward. His introduction of these promises from the past creates a sense of anticipation for what lies ahead. Yes, the reader must understand that the events surrounding these two infants constitute God's long-promised deliverance for Israel. But how God would actually accomplish that deliverance remains to be seen.

One of the crises of our age is finding reliable information. Accusations of fake news echo from both sides of our political and cultural divide. Where can we go to find un-fake news? Studies tell us that young people rely primarily on social media for political news and opinion. God help us. Upon whom can we depend?

Getting trustworthy information was difficult then as well; Luke introduces his gospel in a manner designed to gain the trust of the "most excellent Theophilus" (likely the sponsor for Luke's work). First, Luke explains that he has carefully examined all the evidence regarding Jesus, including information from eyewitnesses (1:1–2). Luke offers an informed explanation of the events. But Luke also states that he will write an "orderly" (1:3) account of Jesus' life. That is, he will put together the story of Jesus in such a way that it highlights the significance of its central figure. As a result, Theophilus can rest assured that what he is about to read is fully reliable.

Informed. Orderly. Reliable. In a word: trustworthy. Luke claims his gospel embodies all of these traits. In Luke's words to Theophilus I hear an appeal for commitment. It's as if Luke says, "You can fully rely on what I am about to tell you. Here is a place to stand. Entrust yourself to the One on whom this message centers."

1. When you think about your life, what or whom do you really rely on?
2. What does trust in God look like in your everyday life?

TWO

Luke 1:5–25

Luke 1:5–25 *In the time of Herod king of Judea there was a priest named Zechariah, who belonged to the priestly division of Abijah; his wife Elizabeth* *was also a descendent of Aaron. [6]Both of them were righteous in the sight of God, observing all the Lord's commands and decrees blamelessly. [7]But they were childless because Elizabeth was not able to conceive, and they were both very old.*

[8]Once when Zechariah's division was on duty and he was serving as priest before God, [9]he was chosen by lot, according to the custom of the priesthood, to go into the temple of the Lord and burn incense. [10]And when the time for the burning of incense came, all the assembled worshipers were praying outside.

[11]Then an angel of the Lord appeared to him, standing at the right side of the altar of incense. [12]When Zechariah saw him, he was startled and was gripped with fear. [13]But the angel said to him: "Do not be afraid, Zechariah; your prayer has been heard. Your wife Elizabeth will bear you a son, and you are to call him John. [14]He will be a joy and delight to you, and many will rejoice because of his birth, [15]for he will be great in the sight of the Lord. He is never to take wine or other fermented drink, and he will be filled with the Holy Spirit even before he is born. [16]He will bring back many of the people of Israel to the Lord their God. [17]And he will go on before the Lord, in the spirit and power of Elijah, to turn the hearts of the parents to their children and the disobedient to the wisdom of the righteous—to make ready a people prepared to the Lord."

[18]Zechariah asked the angel, "How can I be sure of this? I am an old man and my wife is well along in years."

[19]The angel said to him, "I am Gabriel. I stand in the presence of God, and I have been sent to speak to you and to tell you this good news. [20]And now you will be silent and not able to speak until the day this happens, because you did not believe my words, which will come true at their appointed time."

[21]Meanwhile, the people were waiting for Zechariah and wondering why he stayed so long in the temple. [22]When he came out, he could not speak to them. They realized he had seen a vision in the temple, for he kept making signs to them but remained unable to speak.

[23]When his time of service was completed, he returned home. [24]After this his wife Elizabeth became pregnant and for five months remained in seclusion. [25]"The Lord has done this for me," she said. "In these days he has shown his favor and taken away my disgrace among the people."

Key Observation. Common, everyday faithfulness is a prerequisite for service in God's mission.

Understanding the Word. Getting up in the morning was becoming less easy than it once was for Zechariah. His joints ached and the energy he was accustomed to enjoying seemed to run out sooner rather than later. But life was good. Zechariah served as a priest before God in the temple in Jerusalem, an honorable call if there ever was one among his fellow Jews. Furthermore, he and his wife, Elizabeth, were descendants of one of Israel's most significant heroes, the priest Aaron.

Luke gives us additional important information about this couple. We learn that Zechariah served as one among the many priests in the temple, working together in this bustling center of the Jewish world. Luke does not single him out as the chief priest or leader among the priests who served here. Furthermore, Zechariah and Elizabeth are commended as "righteous in the sight of the God," meaning they observed "all the Lord's commands and decrees blamelessly" (v. 6). In other words, these two embodied God's will for his people as called for in Israel's covenant with God. Luke also tells us they were childless. In their context, such a fact would likely have raised eyebrows (1:25). Why has God not given them children? What have they done wrong? Without doubt, as Zechariah's prayer life made apparent (see 1:13), this matter was of great concern to them. All in all, Zechariah and Elizabeth seem like a fairly normal priest and wife, laboring away in the Lord's service.

Yet, God chose to initiate the process of salvation through this faithful but unsuspecting couple. The angel Gabriel appeared to Zechariah and delivered the message that Elizabeth would bear a son. Like Abram and Sarai, God would give him and Elizabeth a child in their old age. But this would be no ordinary child. He would be filled with God's Spirit and, like Elijah, would play a powerful role within God's mission to return Israel to their God.

If I could characterize this priestly couple, I would describe their life as one of common, everyday faithfulness. Even amidst the pain of their childlessness and the shame generated by that fact, they remained blameless before God. Day in and day out, in the normal rhythms of life, they stayed faithful to the Lord. It was *this* couple through whom God chose to work.

We will see this pattern repeated several times in Luke's gospel. God's superstars, those through whom God choose to change the world, often came from among the unnoticed and the unsuspecting rather than those whom the world counted as important. Zechariah and Elizabeth were the first among those so chosen in Luke's gospel.

1. Whom do you know that you would describe as living out common, everyday faithfulness? Why would you characterize them in this manner?
2. Can you name one or two practices or traits that would constitute such faithfulness in your life?

THREE

Luke 1:26–38

Luke 1:26–38 *In the sixth month of Elizabeth's pregnancy, God sent the angel Gabriel to Nazareth, a town in Galilee, [27]to a virgin pledged to be married to a man named Joseph, a descendant of David. The virgin's name was Mary. [28]The angel went to her and said, "Greetings, you who are highly favored! The Lord is with you."*

[29]Mary was greatly troubled at his words and wondered what kind of greeting this might be. [30]But the angel said to her, "Do not be afraid, Mary; you have found favor with God. [31]You will conceive and give birth to a son, and you are to call him Jesus. [32]He will be great and will be called the Son of the Most High. The Lord God will give him the throne of his father David, [33]and he will reign over Jacob's descendants forever; his kingdom will never end."

[34]"How will this be," Mary asked the angel, "since I am a virgin?"

[35]The angel answered, "The Holy Spirit will come on you, and the power of the Most High will overshadow you. So the holy one to be born will be called the Son of God. [36]Even Elizabeth your relative is going to have a child in her old age, and she who was said to be unable to conceive is in her sixth month. [37]For no word from God will ever fail."

[38]"I am the Lord's servant," Mary answered. "May your word to me be fulfilled." Then the angel left her.

Key Observation. Our commitment to God should play out in everyday life, even when it is difficult.

Understanding the Word. Zechariah and Elizabeth were the first couple selected by God to play a role in God's purposes. But it did not take long for God to choose another. Enter Joseph and Mary.

These two couples present a surprising set of contrasts. In both cases, God selected unlikely candidates through whom to bring world-changing children into the world. After all, God first gave a child to Zechariah and Elizabeth, a couple regarded as too old to conceive. Then God selected Joseph and Mary to bear a son, but they were not yet married! Furthermore, God began with a priest serving at the center of the Jewish world, God's own temple in Jerusalem. But he continued with a young peasant woman living in the backwater region of Galilee. Yet these two quite different couples shared an important link—Elizabeth and Mary were related (1:36). Together, these juxtapositions show God's choice of unlikely candidates through whom he would accomplish his salvation. But God's unstoppable plan *would* come to fruition (1:37, 45).

Gabriel was one busy angel. Having appeared to Zechariah in the temple, he then appeared to Mary in Galilee. She must have been dumbfounded. She was just a common young woman in rural Galilee. Still, an *angel of the Lord* appeared to *her*. But that was only the beginning. The angel announced that God himself would give her a son ("What will Mom and Dad say?"). That son would be none other than the long-awaited King from David's line, the One through whom God would restore Israel and bring salvation to the nations. He would be called "Son of the Most High" (a royal title; v. 32) and would be given David's eternal throne (see 2 Samuel 7:11b–16).

Mary's response remains one of the most simple yet profound statements in all of Scripture: "I am the Lord's servant. . . . May your word to me be fulfilled" (v. 38). Understandably, Mary had major questions (1:34). But when push comes to shove, her response to Gabriel and thus to God indicates two significant postures.

Mary's words expressed a deep and profound trust in her God. In effect, she said, "If this, as crazy as it sounds, is truly God's purpose and design, so be it. Count me in!" Additionally, her faith was not just some sort of mere sentiment. Mary's response to Gabriel stated that she was *willing and available* for God's purposes. And that is no small commitment. To entrust herself to God in this manner means she walked away from this encounter with a different life before her. She could no longer go back to who and what she was before.

Obviously, her pregnancy would raise serious questions with Joseph, family, and friends. But even more so, her own child would become King of Israel, the One through whom God would restore the nation.

Mary's deep faith, expressed in her concrete commitment to walk out that faith in all aspects of her life no matter the cost, stands as a challenging example to us all.

1. Have you ever been in a situation that was totally unexpected? How did you learn (or not learn) to trust God in the midst of that situation?

2. In what concrete, practical ways do you or could you demonstrate trust and availability to God in your current circumstances?

FOUR

Luke 1:46–55

Luke 1:46–55 *And Mary said: "My soul glorifies the Lord* [47]*and my spirit rejoices in God my Savior,* [48]*for he has been mindful of the humble state of his servant. From now on all generations will call me blessed,* [49]*for the Mighty One has done great things for me—holy is his name.* [50]*His mercy extends to those who fear him, from generation to generation.* [51]*He has performed might deeds with his arm; he has scattered those who are proud in their inmost thoughts.* [52]*He has brought down rulers from their thrones but has lifted up the humble.* [53]*He has filled the hungry with good things but has sent the rich away empty.* [54]*He has helped his servant Israel, remembering to be merciful* [55]*to Abraham and his descendants forever, just as he promised our ancestors."*

Key Observation. God's demonstrated character in our lives provides reason for thanksgiving and praise.

Understanding the Word. After hearing that her cousin Elizabeth was pregnant (1:36), Mary traveled to see her in Judea. Upon Mary's arrival, a series of three events took place. Together, they dominate this passage.

When Mary greeted Elizabeth, the baby John in Elizabeth's womb leapt for joy (1:41, 44). This surprising development in the story demonstrates

God's deep, personal involvement in the lives of these two women and their unborn sons. Then, although the unborn John could not speak for himself, Elizabeth, filled with the Holy Spirit (1:41), interpreted John's response: Mary, her baby, and Elizabeth herself were all blessed by God. But among these three the emphasis lay on Mary. Not only was she blessed among all women (1:42), she was characterized as one "who has believed that the Lord would fulfill his promises to her!" (1:45). *Elizabeth, speaking prophetically, acknowledged Mary's great trust in God.*

In response to these first two events, Mary broke into one of the greatest bursts of praise in all of the New Testament. Known in Christian tradition as the *Magnificat*, this song belongs alongside many of the Psalms as one of Scripture's greatest acclamations of God's wondrous goodness.

Three themes permeate its content. One, Mary emphasized God's character. God is holy and the Mighty One who performs awesome deeds; God remains faithful, showing mercy on Abraham's descendants; and God demonstrates his justice by scattering the proud and lifting up the humble.

Two, on the basis of God's demonstrated character, Mary unleashed a torrent of thanksgiving, praise, and worship. In a memorable line, she exclaimed, "My soul glorifies the Lord and my spirit rejoices in God my Savior" (1:46–47).

Three, Mary's account of God's character and the worship it provokes highlights key themes that will form the backbone of Luke's account of God's saving actions in Jesus Christ. We will see these themes repeated again and again in Luke's gospel: God extends his mercy through mighty deeds, and those deeds will involve a thoroughgoing reversal of the present order; the proud, the rich, and the rulers will be brought down while the humble will be lifted up and the hungry fed.

This great song demonstrates that Mary saw her life from a larger perspective than just what her circumstances would allow. She was caught up in a much bigger drama of God making all things right if only she would just see it. After all, God's salvation was not a result of Mary's activity and initiative, however much her actions were involved. Rather she was caught up in and participated in what *God* was doing. Her song of praise indicates she understood it perfectly.

1. How do you express your gratitude and wonder for God's faithfulness in your life?
2. In what ways does your understanding of God's character influence how you see your current circumstances?

FIVE

Luke 1:68–79

Luke 1:68–79 *"Praise be to the Lord, the God of Israel, because he has come to his people and redeemed them. [69]He has raised up a horn of salvation for us in the house of his servant David [70](as he said through his holy prophets of long ago), [71]salvation from our enemies and from the hand of all who hate us—[72]to show mercy to our ancestors and to remember his holy covenant, [73]the oath he swore to our father Abraham: [74]to rescue us from the hand of our enemies, and to enable us to serve him without fear [75]in holiness and righteousness before him all our days.*

[76]And you, my child, will be called a prophet of the Most High; for you will go on before the Lord to prepare the way for him, [77]to give his people the knowledge of salvation through the forgiveness of their sins, [78]because of the tender mercy of our God, by which the rising sun will come to us from heaven [79]to shine on those living in darkness and in the shadow of death, to guide our feet into the path of peace."

Key Observation. God should be thanked and praised for his tender mercy enacted in our lives.

Understanding the Word. With the final episode of Luke 1, the anticipated birth of John the Baptist took place. Zechariah named him John as instructed earlier by the angel Gabriel (1:13, 63). In response, and as promised, Zechariah's ability to speak was then restored (1:20, 64).

With his speech regained, Zechariah was immediately filled with the Spirit and prophesized (1:67–79). His words make up the second great song in Luke 1. They fall into two parts.

In verses 68–75 Zechariah praises God for raising up a deliverer for Israel, thus fulfilling promises made to Abraham long ago. Freed from her enemies, Israel will be able to "serve him without fear in holiness and righteousness before him all our days" (1:74b–75).

With the words "And you, my child" in verse 76, Zechariah turned to the second part of his song, a word of prophecy to his son. John would be called a prophet of the Lord. In that role he would do two things. First, he would "prepare the way for the LORD." This imagery comes from the Old Testament prophet Isaiah (40:3). Once in exile from the promised land, Israel's prophets envisioned God's future deliverance of Israel from its enemies in terms of God's original deliverance from enemies: out of bondage, through the wilderness, and into the land of promise. In all of this, God would lead. Malachi also spoke of one who would go before the Lord to prepare Israel for salvation (Malachi 3:1). Zechariah, echoing Gabriel (1:17), said John would occupy this role.

In doing so, John would carry out his second role, namely, giving his people "knowledge of salvation through the forgiveness of their sins" (1:77). In the parallel prophecy regarding John in Luke 1:14–17, the angel Gabriel also spoke of John bringing "back many of the people of Israel to their God" (1:16). In other words, John's ministry would produce repentance from sin. Confronting and dealing with sin lay at the heart of God's purposes for John.

In verses 78–79, Zechariah's prophecy draws all this together by citing the cause of this mighty work God would accomplish through John. It all stems from God's ongoing "tender mercy." Once again, the language of the Old Testament reverberates in Luke's gospel by echoing the language of Psalm 130:7–8. There the psalmist writes, "Israel, put your hope in the LORD, for with the LORD is unfailing love and with him is full redemption. He himself will redeem Israel from all their sins."

The end of this chapter recalls the lyrics of Charles Wesley's great hymn, "Come, Thou Long Expected Jesus."

> Come, thou long expected Jesus,
> Born to set thy people free;
> From our fears and sins release us,
> let us find our rest in thee.

Born thy people to deliver,
born a child and yet a King;
Born to reign in us forever,
Now thy gracious kingdom bring.

1. In what ways have you experienced the tender mercy of God in your life?
2. What appropriate words of praise and thanksgiving can you express to God for his tender mercies showered upon you?

WEEK ONE

GATHERING DISCUSSION OUTLINE

A. **Open session in prayer.** Ask that God would astonish us anew with fresh insight from God's Word and transform us into the disciples that Jesus desires for us to become.

B. **View video for this week's readings.**

C. What were the key insights or takeaways that you gained from your reading during the week and from watching the video commentary? In particular, how did these help you to grow in your faith and understanding of Scripture this week? What parts of the Bible lesson or study raised questions for you?

D. **Discuss selected questions from the daily readings.** Invite class members to share key insights or to raise questions that they found to be the most meaningful.

1. **KEY OBSERVATION:** God's Word, given to us through Luke, can be fully trusted.

   DISCUSSION QUESTION: What does trust in God look like in your everyday life?

2. **KEY OBSERVATION:** Common, everyday faithfulness is a prerequisite for service in God's mission.

   DISCUSSION QUESTION: Whom do you know that you would describe as living out common, everyday faithfulness? Why would you characterize them in this manner?

3. **KEY OBSERVATION:** Our commitment to God should play out in everyday life, even when it is difficult.

   DISCUSSION QUESTION: In what concrete, practical ways do you or could you demonstrate trust and availability to God in your current circumstances?

4. **KEY OBSERVATION:** God's demonstrated character in our lives provides reason for thanksgiving and praise.

   DISCUSSION QUESTION: How do you express your gratitude and wonder for God's faithfulness in your life?

5. **KEY OBSERVATION:** God should be thanked and praised for his tender mercy enacted in our lives.

   DISCUSSION QUESTION: What appropriate words of praise and thanksgiving can you express to God for his tender mercies showered upon you?

E. **As the study concludes, consider specific ways that this week's Bible lesson invites you to grow and calls you to change.** How do this week's scriptures call us to think differently? How do they challenge us to align ourselves with God's work in the world? What specific actions should we take to apply the insights of the lesson into our daily lives? What kind of person does our Bible lesson call us to become?

F. **Close session with prayer.** Emphasize God's ongoing work of transformation in our lives in preparation for loving mission and service in the world. Pray for absent class members as well as for persons whom we need to invite to join our study.

WEEK TWO

Jesus' Preparation for Ministry

ONE

Luke 2:8–20

Luke 2:8–20 ESV *And in the same region there were shepherds out in the field,
keeping watch over their flock by night. [9]And an angel of the Lord appeared to
them, and the glory of the Lord shone around them, and they were filled with
great fear. [10]And the angel said to them, "Fear not, for behold, I bring you good
news of great joy that will be for all the people. [11]For unto you is born this day
in the city of David a Savior, who is Christ the Lord. [12]And this will be a sign for
you: you will find a baby wrapped in swaddling cloths and lying in a manger."
[13]And suddenly there was with the angel a multitude of the heavenly host praising
God and saying, [14]"Glory to God in the highest, and on earth peace among those
with whom he is pleased!"*

*[15]When the angels went away from them into heaven, the shepherds said to
one another, "Let us go over to Bethlehem and see this thing that has happened,
which the Lord has made known to us." [16]And they went with haste and found
Mary and Joseph, and the baby lying in a manger. [17]And when they saw it,
they made known the saying that had been told them concerning this child.
[18]And all who heard it wondered at what the shepherds told them. [19]But Mary
treasured up all these things, pondering them in her heart. [20]And the shepherds
returned, glorifying and praising God for all they had heard and seen, as it had
been told them.*

Key Observation. God can be trusted with our hopes.

Understanding the Word. In Luke 2:1–4:13 we read of the events from Jesus' birth until the final stage of his preparation for ministry. Jesus was born, he was presented to the Lord, John the Baptist began his ministry, and Jesus underwent testing in the wilderness. In recounting these stories, Luke accomplishes two things.

As in Luke 1, he highlights the significance of Jesus within God's mission. Angels appeared. Prophecy of old was fulfilled. Current prophets spoke of the role of this child. And so on. We cannot miss that Jesus stood at the center of what God had planned and was about to accomplish.

Furthermore, Luke tells these stories in a manner that makes us anticipate what was to come in Jesus' ministry itself. For example, when the devout Simeon prophesied that through this infant Jesus, God's salvation had come for all nations (2:30–32), we wonder what this meant and how it would take place. But answers to those questions can only come when we read further into Luke's gospel. This week we will walk our way through these chapters as they get us ready us for Jesus' ministry to come.

As I noted previously, the preparations for Jesus' birth involved a number of supernatural events. The angel Gabriel appeared to Mary with astounding news that she, a virgin, would give birth to a child by the power of God (1:26–38). When Mary met her cousin Elizabeth, Elizabeth was filled with the Holy Spirit and pronounced Mary and her coming child blessed (1:39–45).

Once Mary's child was born, supernatural events continued. In this case, an angel appeared to shepherds and announced that the Savior, Christ the Lord, had been born in Bethlehem. A number of angels then appeared to these shepherds, singing praise to God.

One wonders what Joseph and Mary thought about all of this. After all, this wasn't the normal pattern of life for Galilean commoners like themselves (or anyone else for that matter). What could all this mean? How could *they* of all people be caught up in something God was up to?

Luke gives us a brief glimpse into Mary's mind-set. When the shepherds go to Bethlehem as instructed, they find Joseph, Mary, and the baby about whom all this heavenly fuss had been made. Hearing this, Mary "treasured up all these things, pondering them in her heart" (2:19).

We've already been told that when the angel Gabriel first told Mary of her role in what God was about to do, she said, in effect, "I'm in!" (1:38). After further supernatural events surrounded the birth of her son, she once again placed her faith and hope in the Lord. She treasured what God had revealed about this baby and waited for how God would bring this all about in God's timing. The fulfillment of God's word hadn't all happened yet. But Mary's hope in the Lord was firm.

1. What hopes do you hold for God's work for you or for your family?
2. What would a posture of hope look like as you live it out?

TWO

Luke 2:27–35

Luke 2:27–35 ESV *And he came in the Spirit into the temple, and when the parents brought in the child Jesus, to do for him according to the custom of the Law, [28]he took him up in his arms and blessed God and said, [29]"Lord, now you are letting your servant depart in peace, according to your word; [30]for my eyes have seen your salvation [31]that you have prepared in the presence of all peoples, [32]a light for revelation to the Gentiles, and for glory to your people Israel."*

[33]And his father and his mother marveled at what was said about him. [34]And Simeon blessed them and said to Mary his mother, "Behold, this child is appointed for the fall and rising of many in Israel, and for a sign that is opposed [35](and a sword will pierce through your own soul also), so that thoughts from many hearts may be revealed."

Key Observation. Following Jesus does not exempt us from problems.

Understanding the Word. In Luke 2:22–39, Mary and Joseph present Jesus to God in the Jerusalem temple. In doing so, they encounter Simeon. In Luke's retelling of their meeting, we see important themes from Luke 1 return again. For example, all three adults display devout character similar to that of Zechariah and Elizabeth. Zechariah and Elizabeth are characterized as upright before God and blameless with regard to God's commandments (1:7). In chapter 2, Luke notes that Joseph and Mary faithfully take Jesus to the temple for purification just "as it is written in the Law of the Lord" (2:23–24). Furthermore, Simeon is singled out as "righteous and devout" (2:25). Truly, these were trustworthy, faithful people.

Luke also notes, as in chapter 1, the continued working of the Holy Spirit. Within a mere three verses (2:25–27), Luke mentions the Holy Spirit in relation to Simeon three times. Luke's emphasis on the work of the Spirit provides one more indicator of the profound significance of these people and the events in which they were caught up.

At the center of this passage stand Simeon and his blessing of Joseph and Mary. Luke characterizes Simeon in a manner that prepares us to feel the impact of his words; he is "righteous and devout" and the Holy Spirit is upon him (2:25). But, Luke also tells us he waited for the "consolation of Israel" (2:26), words that recall Isaiah's prophecy of Israel's deliverance (Isaiah 40:1–2; 49:13). Finally, the Holy Spirit had revealed to him that he would not die before he saw "the Lord's Christ" (ESV) or "Messiah" (2:26).

Simeon's message to Joseph and Mary consisted of thanksgiving to God for the child plus a prediction about the coming impact of Jesus' life. Let's look at both elements.

First, Simeon gives thanks that he has been allowed to see God's "salvation" (v. 30). Jesus as a bringer of divine salvation is a theme unique to Luke. As with the term "consolation," it refers to God's deliverance of Israel and the nations from their rebellion against God.

But second, after blessing the couple (1:34), Simeon spoke a troubling word to Mary (1:34–35). He predicted that Jesus would cause division within Israel, provoking opposition against himself. Furthermore, Mary would experience great sorrow as a result of what happens to Jesus. The reader who knows how the gospel ends understands all too well of what Simeon speaks.

We've already seen that Mary had proven to be a model of faithfulness to God. Then she learns that the journey upon which she and her child have begun will cost her dearly. Faithfulness to God within the purposes of God do not exempt her from life pain.

Our pain incurred in following Jesus will be far less than Mary experienced. We are more likely to face social ostracism, though in some cases jobs and livelihoods could be threatened. But, like Mary, following Jesus does not exempt us from difficulty.

1. In what ways do you find following Jesus difficult?
2. By what means do you find encouragement to faithfully follow Jesus in spite of problems you encounter?

THREE

Luke 3:1–14

Luke 3:1–14 ESV *In the fifteenth year of the reign of Tiberias Caesar, Pontius Pilate being governor of Judea, and Herod being tetrarch of Galilee, and his brother Philip tetrarch of the region of Ituraea and Trachonitis, and Lysanias tetrarch of Abilene, [2]during the high priesthood of Annas and Caiaphas, the word of God came to John the son of Zechariah in the wilderness. [3]And he went into all the region around the Jordan, proclaiming a baptism of repentance for the forgiveness of sins. [4]As it is written in the book of the words of Isaiah the prophet, "The voice of one crying in the wilderness: 'Prepare the way of the Lord, make his paths straight. [5]Every valley shall be filled, and every mountain and hill shall be made low, and the crooked shall become straight, and the rough places shall become level ways, [6]and all flesh shall see the salvation of God.'"*

[7]He said therefore to the crowds that came out to be baptized by him, "You brood of vipers! Who warned you to flee from the wrath to come? [8]Bear fruits in keeping with repentance. And do not begin to say to yourselves, 'We have Abraham as our father.' For I tell you, God is able from these stones to raise up children for Abraham. [9]Even now the axe is laid to the root of the trees. Every tree therefore that does not bear good fruit is cut down and thrown into the fire."

[10]And the crowds asked him, "What then shall we do?" [11]And he answered them, "Whoever has two tunics is to share with him who has none, and whoever has food is to do likewise." [12]Tax collectors also came to be baptized and said to him, "Teacher, what shall we do?" [13]And he said to them, "Collect no more than you are authorized to do." [14]Soldiers also asked him, "And we, what shall we do?" And he said to them, "Do not extort money from anyone by threats or by false accusation, and be content with your wages."

Key Observation. Repentance is the necessary prerequisite for forgiveness of our sin.

Understanding the Word. This episode opens with two of my favorite verses in all of Scripture. They are often overlooked because they merely set the stage for Luke's description of John the Baptist's message and ministry. But within Luke's gospel, they embody a key element of his understanding of God's good news.

Luke begins by providing a Who's Who of the so-called important people in the world. He names the Roman emperor and the chief Roman officials exercising political authority in ancient Palestine (3:1). He goes on to name high priests ruling over the Jewish people, Annas and Caiaphas (3:2a). But once he completes this catalog of key figures in the world of that time, he turns to the work of God—and it involves *none* of them. Rather, *the word of God* comes to an insignificant figure (John the son of Zechariah) in an insignificant place (in the wilderness; 3:2b). As Mary sang earlier, "[God] has brought down the mighty from their thrones and has exalted those of humble estate" (1:52 ESV).

And what is the word of God that came to John? Luke summarizes John's message by quoting Isaiah 40:3–5,

> A voice cries:
> "In the wilderness prepare the way of the LORD;
> make straight in the desert a highway for our God.
> Every valley shall be lifted up,
> and every mountain and hill be made low.
> the uneven ground shall become level,
> and the rough places a plain.
> And the glory of the LORD shall be revealed,
> and all flesh shall see it together,
> for the mouth of the LORD has spoken." (ESV)

These words come from the opening verses of the section of Isaiah where the prophet looks forward to a future day when God will restore the kingdom to Israel. For centuries Israel's hope for God's coming deliverance had been fueled by these chapters in Isaiah. By citing just a few verses from their beginning, Luke invokes Isaiah's vision in its entirety.

Note that while Luke cites Isaiah's positive words of *hope* he characterizes John's messages in fairly negative terms. John went around "preaching a baptism of repentance" (v. 3). John exclaims, "You brood of vipers! Who warned you to flee from the coming wrath? . . . The ax is already at the root of the trees, and every tree that does not produce good fruit will be cut down and thrown into fire" (3:7, 9).

Still, John connects repentance with forgiveness: repentance is "for the forgiveness of sins" (v. 3). Without repentance there is no forgiveness. Without repentance and forgiveness, there is no salvation. John's message prepared the way for what Jesus would bring.

This episode continues Luke's clarion announcement that the time for Israel's salvation had come with the arrival of John and Jesus. But with John's ministry we learn that Israel's experience of this saving work of God hinges upon Israel's repentance. And so the experience of God's saving work has remained to this day. Repentance entails a turning *from* self-centered modes of life *toward* full surrender to God's rule in our life. See how concrete it makes this for those who heard John's message: share what you have, do not cheat others, and so on. True repentance involves concrete acts of turning *from* as well as turning *to*.

1. What concrete behavior or attitude could you repent *from*?
2. What behavior would demonstrate a concrete act of turning *to* Jesus' rule over your life?

FOUR

Luke 3:21–38

Luke 3:21–38 ESV *Now when all the people were baptized, and when Jesus also had been baptized and was praying, the heavens were opened, [22]and the Holy Spirit descended on him in bodily form, like a dove; and a voice came from heaven, "You are my beloved Son; with you I am well pleased."*

[23]Jesus, when he began his ministry, was about thirty years of age, being the son (as was supposed) of Joseph, the son of Heli, [24]the son of Matthat, the son of Levi, the son of Melchi, the son of Jannai, the son of Joseph, [25]the son of Mattathias, the son of Amos, the son of Nahum, the son of Esli, the son of Naggai, [26]the son of Maath, the son of Mattathias, the son of Semein, the son of Josech, the son of Joda, [27]the son of Joanan, the son of Rhesa, the son of Zerubbabel, the son of Shealtiel, the son of Neri, [28]the son of Melchi, the son of Addi, the son of

Cosam, the son of Elmadam, the son of Er, [29]the son of Joshua, the son of Eliezer,
the son of Jorim, the son of Matthat, the son of Levi, [30]the son of Simeon, the
son of Judah, the son of Joseph, the son of Jonam, the son of Eliakim, [31]the son
of Melea, the son of Menna, the son of Mattatha, the son of Nathan, the son of
David, [32]the son of Jesse, the son of Obed, the son of Boaz, the son of Sala, the
son of Nahshon, [33]the son of Amminadab, the son of Admin, the son of Arni,
the son of Hezron, the son of Perez, the son of Judah, [34]the son of Jacob, the son
of Isaac, the son of Abraham, the son of Terah, the son of Nahor, [35]the son of
Serug, the son of Reu, the son of Peleg, the son of Eber, the son of Shelah, [36]the
son of Cainan, the son of Arphaxad, the son of Shem, the son of Noah, the son
of Lamech, [37]the son of Methuselah, the son of Enoch, the son of Jared, the son
of Mahalaleel, the son of Cainan, [38]the son of Enos, the son of Seth, the son of
Adam, the son of God.

Key Observation. Your identity shapes your life in profound ways.

Understanding the Word. The genealogies found throughout the Bible typically serve as sections of Scripture we just skip over. Come on! You know you've done it!

But while all the details of who was whose son may seem unimportant to us, the genealogy in Luke 3 actually plays an important role within his gospel. At Jesus' baptism, immediately preceding Luke's recitation of Jesus' ancestors, a voice from heaven makes a solemn pronouncement over Jesus as he emerges from the Jordan River, "You are my Son, whom I love; with you I am well pleased" (3:22). Luke then begins and ends Jesus' genealogy with reminders of precisely this point: Jesus is God's Son. He begins the genealogy with Joseph, but prefaces his naming of Joseph with the comments that Jesus "being the son (as was supposed) of Joseph" (3:23 ESV). In other words, Jesus' family and neighbors thought of him as Joseph's son. But Luke acknowledges that we as readers know better. The Holy Spirit came over Mary and she conceived Jesus (1:31–35). Luke then ends his genealogy by tracing Jesus' lineage to God himself: "the son of Adam, the son of God" (3:38).

All of this serves to affirm who Jesus is. Jesus' divine sonship was first spoken to Mary by Gabriel (1:32, 35). As we have just seen, it was proclaimed again by a voice from heaven itself. Luke's repetition of this fact for a third time reinforces and legitimates Jesus' calling within God's mission: he will bring salvation to Israel and reign over Israel forever.

In many parts of the world today, genealogies provide a sense of identity just like they did in the ancient world. When I taught in East Africa for many years, students often found the Bible's genealogies fascinating because, in their cultures, knowing one's ancestors played a crucial role in one's self-understanding.

Such family connections are not strange for us. As a teenager in the rural Midwest, I ran in a track meet in a small town not far away from my own. After I crossed the finish line in my heat, I went back to the man keeping time and gave him my name so he could record my time. He looked at me and asked, "Are you E. B. Miller's grandson?" When I answered yes, I recall instantly feeling I needed to be on my best behavior. I wasn't just some kid running a hurdles race. I was part of a family. With that identity came expectations that I did not want to disappoint. Even in the individualistic United States, our family identity influences how we live in profound ways.

What tells you who you are? Where is your identity rooted? One of the foremost identifiers of followers of Jesus found in the Bible is that we are part of *God's* family. We are *God's* children. Who we understand ourselves to be determines how we live in profound ways.

1. Can you recall a moment when you realized what made you *you*? Where do you find your identity? Family? Work? Ethnicity or race?

2. How does your identity shape what you value and how you live in relationship with others? If you are a follower of Jesus, how does that all-encompassing identity shape who you are?

FIVE

Luke 4:1–13

Luke 4:1–13 ESV *And Jesus, full of the Holy Spirit, returned from the Jordan and was led by the Spirit in the wilderness* [2]*for forty days, being tempted by the devil. And he ate nothing during those days. And when they were ended, he was hungry.* [3]*The devil said to him, "If you are the Son of God, command this stone*

to become bread." 4And Jesus answered him, "It is written, 'Man shall not live by
bread alone.'" 5And the devil took him up and showed him all the kingdoms of the
world in a moment of time, 6and said to him, "To you I will give all this authority
and their glory, for it has been delivered to me, and I give it to whom I will. 7If
you, then, will worship me, it will all be yours." 8And Jesus answered him, "It is
written, "'You shall worship the Lord you God, and him only shall you serve.'"

9And he took him to Jerusalem and set him on the pinnacle of the temple and
said to him, "If you are the Son of God, throw yourself down from here, 10for it is
written, "'He will command his angels concerning you, to guard you.' 11and "'On
their hands they will bear you up, lest you strike your foot against a stone.'"

12And Jesus answered him, "It is said, 'You shall not put the Lord your God
to the test.'" 13And when the devil had ended every temptation, he departed from
him until an opportune time.

Key Observation. We resist the devil's schemes against us by knowing and holding to God's promises to us.

Understanding the Word. One last event awaited Jesus before his ministry began: he was tempted (or as it's sometimes translated, "tested") three times by Satan in the wilderness. Luke prefaces his descriptions of these temptations by making two important points. First, Jesus did not go to the wilderness helplessly. The Spirit empowered (or "filled") him. Second, the Spirit led him to the place where all this would happen. In other words, facing these temptations was not some mistaken sidestep in the process of Jesus living into his call within God's mission. Rather, it served as a necessary step before Jesus launched into ministry.

As the temptations took place, Jesus was vulnerable. He spent forty days in the wilderness without eating. Obviously, as Luke says, Jesus was hungry (4:2). Furthermore, he was alone with no one to observe his actions. What happened in the wilderness could stay in the wilderness (or so Jesus could have thought). Hungry and alone, temptation could become, shall we say, ever more tempting.

We can observe patterns in Luke's bare bones descriptions of these events. In two of the temptations, the devil appealed to Jesus' identity, "If you are the *Son of God* [and you really are] . . ." (4:3, 9, emphasis added). In other words, the devil tried to get Jesus to reason on the basis of who Jesus truly is. Jesus withstood all three offers from the devil by quoting Scripture (4:4, 8, 12).

The focal point of the temptations lay in whether Jesus would follow the Spirit in trusting God or use his status as God's Son to seek his own ends. Thus, the devil first tempted Jesus to use his power to end his hunger. Next, the devil offered Jesus worldwide power and glory if only Jesus would worship him. Finally, the devil pulled out all the stops and tempted Jesus using God's promise of protection in Scripture (Ps. 91). If Jesus threw himself from the top of the temple surely God would protect him, wouldn't he? But Jesus proved faithful to God, refusing to put God to the test (Deut. 6:16).

Jesus successfully turned away the devil. His ministry would then begin in earnest. But we can learn much from Jesus' encounter with the devil in these verses.

The devil attacked Jesus when he was vulnerable. Jesus was hungry. Whatever the devil was offering, it would have dealt with Jesus' immediate pain. Jesus was also alone. No one was nearby to hold him accountable.

But what the devil offered was a mirage. If I ever get as hungry as Jesus was, the potential taste of bread will sound really good. But the devil's bread, once consumed, will turn to dust. What the devil offers will not turn out as promised.

In the end, Jesus successfully defeated the devil's plans to corrupt him by clinging to God's promises.

1. In what situations are you most vulnerable to temptation to disobey God?
2. What scripture can you memorize that will constantly remind you of God's love and purposes?

WEEK TWO

GATHERING DISCUSSION OUTLINE

A. **Open session in prayer.** Ask that God would astonish us anew with fresh insight from God's Word and transform us into the disciples that Jesus desires for us to become.

B. **View video for this week's readings.**

C. What were the key insights or takeaways that you gained from your reading during the week and from watching the video commentary? In particular, how did these help you to grow in your faith and understanding of Scripture this week? What parts of the Bible lesson or study raised questions for you?

D. **Discuss selected questions from the daily readings.** Invite class members to share key insights or to raise questions that they found to be the most meaningful.

1. **KEY OBSERVATION:** God can be trusted with our hopes.

   DISCUSSION QUESTION: What would a posture of hope look like as you live it out?

2. **KEY OBSERVATION:** Following Jesus does not exempt us from problems.

   DISCUSSION QUESTION: By what means do you find encouragement to faithfully follow Jesus in spite of problems you encounter?

3. **KEY OBSERVATION:** Repentance is the necessary prerequisite for forgiveness of our sin.

   DISCUSSION QUESTION: What behavior would demonstrate a concrete act of turning *to* Jesus' rule over your life?

4. **KEY OBSERVATION:** Your identity shapes your life in profound ways.

   DISCUSSION QUESTION: How does your identity shape what you value and how you live in relationship with others? If you are a follower of Jesus, how does that all-encompassing identity shape who you are?

5. **KEY OBSERVATION:** We resist the devil's schemes against us by knowing and holding to God's promises to us.

   DISCUSSION QUESTION: What scripture can you memorize that will constantly remind you of God's love and purposes?

E. **As the study concludes, consider specific ways that this week's Bible lesson invites you to grow and calls you to change.** How do this week's scriptures call us to think differently? How do they challenge us to align ourselves with God's work in the world? What specific actions should we take to apply the insights of the lesson into our daily lives? What kind of person does our Bible lesson call us to become?

F. **Close session with prayer.** Emphasize God's ongoing work of transformation in our lives in preparation for loving mission and service in the world. Pray for absent class members as well as for persons whom we need to invite to join our study.

WEEK THREE

Jesus Begins His Ministry

ONE

Luke 4:14–21 (Part One)

Luke 4:14–21 NRSV *Then Jesus, filled with the power of the Spirit, returned to Galilee, and a report about him spread through all the surrounding country. [15]He began to teach in their synagogues and was praised by everyone.*

[16]When he came to Nazareth, where he had been brought up, he went to the synagogue on the sabbath day, as was his custom. He stood up to read, [17]and the scroll of the prophet Isaiah was given to him. He unrolled the scroll and found the place where it was written: [18]"The Spirit of the Lord is upon me, because he has anointed me to bring good news to the poor. He has sent me to proclaim release to the captives and recovery of sight to the blind, to let the oppressed go free, [19]to proclaim the year of the Lord's favor."

[20]And he rolled up the scroll, gave it back to the attendant, and sat down. The eyes of all in the synagogue were fixed on him. [21]Then he began to say to them, "Today this scripture has been fulfilled in your hearing."

Key Observation. For Jesus, Scripture played a central role in understanding and living into his role in God's mission. God, speaking through Scripture, can do the same for us.

Understanding the Word. Full of the Holy Spirit, Jesus had successfully resisted the devil's temptations in the wilderness (4:1–13). Preparations for ministry were complete. Jesus, still empowered by the Spirit, returned to Galilee, where he began to teach in Jewish synagogues. Jesus had launched his ministry in earnest.

This week we examine Jesus' activity as his work commences. What he says and does in these passages sets the agenda for all that follows. Therefore, wisdom dictates that we study these events carefully. In particular, we need to examine the events surrounding Jesus' first sermon in his hometown of Nazareth.

Jesus began by quoting Isaiah 61:1–2. In doing so, this passage defines both who Jesus is as well as the purpose of his ministry.

Jesus claimed that Isaiah 61 speaks of him. He explained the significance of that identification through four purpose statements ("*to bring . . . to proclaim . . . to let . . . to proclaim*"). Let's briefly summarize these four purposes in two points.

First, the primary target of Jesus' proclamation would be the *poor*. In the context of ancient Palestine, the poor would include not just the economically deprived; it would also involve those socially marginalized. We can see these people identified here: the captives, the blind, and the oppressed. Jesus would bring good news to the social outcasts.

Second, Jesus' ministry would affect *release* for captives and for the oppressed (the idea of release is used for both groups). As we will see in Luke's gospel, release would come to those captive to demonic powers, to economic bondage, and to physical impairment. But the term is also used for *forgiveness* of sins (1:77; 3:3; 24:47). *Release* thus becomes an all-encompassing term for the outcome of Jesus' work.

The guarantee of the effectiveness for both of these purposes is the work of the Spirit. Beginning in 3:21 and continuing until this point in the narrative, Luke has emphasized the role of God's Spirit in relation to Jesus. The Holy Spirit descended on Jesus (3:22). Jesus was filled with and led by the Spirit (4:1). Jesus left the wilderness still filled with the Spirit and entered Galilee (4:14). Jesus stated the divine nature of his calling and mission, "The Spirit of the Lord is upon me, because he has anointed me" (4:18 NRSV).

What all this points to is the role of Scripture in Jesus' self-understanding. If we were to ask Jesus who he is, what he is doing, and why is he doing it, he would answer (as here) from Scripture. We've already seen Jesus rely upon the truths found in Scripture to do battle with the devil. Then Jesus defined his identity and his mission on the basis of Isaiah. For Jesus, then, Scripture played the central role in understanding and living into his God-given and empowered role within God's purpose.

1. Why should God's Word shape our self-understanding?
2. How can you create a way to read Scripture regularly?

TWO

Luke 4:14–21 (Part Two)

Luke 4:14–21 NRSV *Then Jesus, filled with the power of the Spirit, returned to Galilee, and a report about him spread through all the surrounding country.* [15]*He began to teach in their synagogues and was praised by everyone.*

[16]*When he came to Nazareth, where he had been brought up, he went to the synagogue on the sabbath day, as was his custom. He stood up to read,* [17]*and the scroll of the prophet Isaiah was given to him. He unrolled the scroll and found the place where it was written:* [18]*"The Spirit of the Lord is upon me, because he has anointed me to bring good news to the poor. He has sent me to proclaim release to the captives and recovery of sight to the blind, to let the oppressed go free,* [19]*to proclaim the year of the Lord's favor."*

[20]*And he rolled up the scroll, gave it back to the attendant, and sat down. The eyes of all in the synagogue were fixed on him.* [21]*Then he began to say to them, "Today this scripture has been fulfilled in your hearing."*

Key Observation. Jesus' ministry primarily focused on those who had no one else to help them. In doing so, he set the pattern for our own lives as we follow him.

Understanding the Word. Jesus claimed that God anointed him and empowered him through the Holy Spirit for specific purposes. The primary target for his ministry would be the *poor*. The fundamental effect of that ministry would be one of *release*. Today we look at both within the context of Luke. Keep in mind that this quotation from Isaiah 61:1–2 functions as a summary of Jesus' ministry. Luke will spell out the key parts of that general statement in the rest of his gospel.

Jesus' call consists of bringing "good news to the poor." At first glance, Jesus' call to bring good news to the *poor* makes it sound as though he limited his ministry only to those with no economic resources. Within the social realities of Jesus' day, however, a host of factors made one poor. These include family history, religious purity, illness, and so on. Jesus, using Isaiah 61, names such people in verse 18: the captives, the blind, and the oppressed.

When we look at those whom Jesus helps in Luke's gospel, we will see people in precisely these categories. For example, in the passage that immediately follows these events in Nazareth (4:31–37), Jesus cast an unclean spirit out of a man. In 7:21–22 we hear of Jesus giving sight to the blind. In all of these incidents (and there are many in Luke), we find people poor for a variety of reasons. Jesus *released* them.

If *release* characterizes the effect of Jesus' ministry, that term could also refer to the forgiveness of sins. In 7:36–50, Jesus forgave a "sinful woman" who anointed him with oil. According to the description of the woman, we can see she was a social outcast. That's why Jesus' interaction with her caused such a fuss. But Jesus *released* her through forgiveness.

What these episodes hold in common is that Jesus reached out to those who have no one else to help them. These were the poor of whom Jesus spoke.

What would such people look like in our context? Examples abound. We know people who do emergency foster care for children. The need arises in cases of domestic abuse, emergency illness, or the arrest of a parent when no family is available to help.

Others help people getting out of prison to get back on their feet. Studies show that unless a newly released prisoner finds food, shelter, and a job within seventy-two hours of his or her release, that person runs a 90 percent chance of ending up back in jail. These saints work with prisoners preparing to be released in order to address these needs.

The list of such poor within our reach could go on and on. Following in Jesus' footsteps, we have endless opportunities to carry on the ministry Jesus announced in Nazareth.

1. Among the large numbers of people you encounter on a weekly basis, who would count among the poor? What steps could you take to help them?

2. If you cannot think of any poor people you encounter regularly, what could you choose to do so that you can begin to engage the poor in your community?

THREE

Luke 4:31–37

Luke 4:31–37 NRSV *He went down to Capernaum, a city in Galilee, and was teaching them on the sabbath. [32]They were astounded at his teaching, because he spoke with authority. [33]In the synagogue there was a man who had the spirit of an unclean demon, and he cried out with a loud voice, [34]"Let us alone! What have you to do with us, Jesus of Nazareth? Have you come to destroy us? I know who you are, the Holy One of God." [35]But Jesus rebuked him, saying, "Be silent, and come out of him!" When the demon had thrown him down before them, he came out of him without having done him any harm. [36]They were all amazed and kept saying to one another, "What kind of utterance is this? For with authority and power he commands the unclean spirits, and out they come!" [37]And a report about him began to reach every place in the region.*

Key Observation. Doing life right depends on allowing Jesus to be the ultimate authority in our lives.

Understanding the Word. Jesus' authority formed one of his distinctive, defining features. He taught authoritatively (4:32). He commanded "unclean spirits" (4:36). He was able to forgive sins (5:24). Jesus even had authority over nature (8:25). As a result, people responded to Jesus with amazement and they followed him.

In our day, authority gets a bad name for a number of reasons. Most of us experience some degree of misused authority. We have a boss who expects us to work evenings and weekends even when we receive no compensation for the additional labor. Or we lived under the thumb of an overbearing parent. But whether at home or at work, we came to view anyone with authority over us with suspicion.

Our drive to be independent forms one of the defining features of our culture. We don't want anyone telling *us* what to do! The heroes and heroines that fill Disney movies are such characters. For example, recall how the Little Mermaid defies her father. In the end, she wins out and her father changes his mind.

We make a serious mistake if we think of authority only as something negative. Rightful, godly authority is properly exercised for the protection and life-giving holy empowerment of others. I pray that I exercise my rightful authority as a parent in a manner that encourages my children to love God and walk in God's ways. How much more concern do you think God has for our good?

God isn't here to spoil our party. As our Creator and Redeemer, God seeks to give us life in its fullness. But that requires that we submit our lives to the rightful authority of Jesus. Left to our own devices (doing it our way), we'll make a mess of it.

The notion that we can escape authority is false. Living under authority is simply part of life. As children, we had parents and teachers. As adults, our job places us under someone else. Life cannot be lived out from under such structures. The issue, then, isn't whether or not we will live under authority. The question is: To which authority will we submit?

In the passage for today, the unclean demon recognized Jesus' authority and power: "Have you come to destroy us?" But the demon also understood that Jesus could do this because of who Jesus was (and is), "the Holy One of God." In other words, *Jesus has rightful, ultimate authority.*

For us the questions remain: Will I allow Jesus to organize my life? Will I allow Jesus to determine priorities in my life? Or will I insist on doing it my way?

1. Who or what do you think exerts authority over your life and decisions?
2. What would be one practical way you could submit your life to Jesus today?

FOUR

Luke 4:38–39

Luke 4:38–39 NRSV *After leaving the synagogue he entered Simon's house. Now Simon's mother-in-law was suffering from a high fever, and they asked him about her.* [39]*Then he stood over her and rebuked the fever, and it left her. Immediately she got up and began to serve them.*

Key Observation. At its heart, following Jesus necessitates serving others.

Understanding the Word. This brief episode easily gets lost in the action-packed narrative of Luke 4. Think about it. The devil tempted Jesus three times (4:1–13). Jesus then entered the synagogue in his hometown, announced the purpose of his ministry, and nearly got himself killed in the process (4:14–30). Finally, he cast out demons and attracted huge crowds (4:31–44). In the midst of all this, Luke inserts this short episode involving Jesus, his disciples, and Peter's mother-in-law. But what it lacks in length and drama (no crowds, no demons), it makes up for in importance.

Note the patterns running through these stories. For example, the healing of Peter's mother-in-law occurs in a series of healing and deliverance stories. Jesus just cast out a demon (Luke 4:31–37). In what follows, Luke will tell us of Jesus healing "all" who were sick and brought to him (4:40). Jesus will also rebuke and cast out many demons (4:41).

In each case, Luke also reports the responses to what Jesus did. In the first instance, people responded in awe of Jesus and his authority (4:36). As a result, word of Jesus' activities "began to reach every place in the region" (4:37 NRSV). Later, the demons shouted, "You are the Son of God!" Luke indicates they did this because they knew Jesus was the Messiah (4:41). In other words, Luke draws our attention to the consistent, spectacular nature of responses to Jesus.

In the midst of all this, we read about Peter's mother-in-law. The healing itself sounds much like other healing stories in Luke. Someone told Jesus about the condition. Jesus then "stood over her and rebuked the fever" and it went away (4:39 NRSV). So far, nothing out of the ordinary.

But her response seems all out of line with the others in this section. Elsewhere demons shouted Jesus' identity or crowds responded with utter amazement. Peter's mother-in-law simply got up from her bed immediately and began to serve those in the house.

We could read this as just another example of a woman having to do a woman's work in the ancient world. She couldn't tell others about Jesus. She had to cook! But given the patterns among Luke's stories in this chapter, I don't think that is what Luke is trying to tell us. Responses to Jesus are important. In this case, her first act as a Jesus-healed person was to *serve* others. Right in the midst of a series of entirely appropriate (and somewhat spectacular) reactions to Jesus, we find Peter's mother-in-law responding by doing *the* characteristic activity of a Jesus-following person: serving others.

This other-directed orientation of Peter's mother-in-law reflected the pattern lived out by Jesus himself. In Mark's gospel, Jesus said it this way: "the Son of Man came not to be served but to serve, and to give his life a ransom for many" (Mark 10:45 NRSV). Of all the responses to Jesus in this chapter, this woman's was the most in alignment with Jesus' own way of living.

1. What one action could you take today that would benefit others rather than yourself?
2. How can you make serving others a consist pattern of life?

FIVE

Luke 4:42–44

Luke 4:42–44 NRSV *At daybreak he departed and went into a deserted place.*
And the crowds were looking for him; and when they reached him, they wanted
to prevent him from leaving them. [43]*But he said to them, "I must proclaim the*
good news of the kingdom of God to the other cities also; for I was sent for this
purpose." [44]*So he continued proclaiming the message in the synagogues of Judea.*

Key Observation. Life as God intends is found only in submission to God our King.

Understanding the Word. Early on in Jesus' ministry, he pointed out that at the core of his calling stood the task of proclaiming the kingdom of God. If you read through Luke, you'll see the subject of the kingdom come up again and again. In fact, Luke mentions the "kingdom of God" thirty-one times and refers to the same simply as "kingdom" another seven times. Without question, God's kingdom stands at the heart of what Luke tells us about Jesus.

But what is the kingdom of God? Nowhere did Jesus give us a straight definition. He did say it can be proclaimed (9:60) and that it can come near (10:9, 11). He instructed us to pray for it to come (11:2). He also used stories in parable form to tell us what the kingdom is like. It grows like a mustard seed (13:18–19) or spreads like leaven in flour (13:20–21). In other words, despite its importance, we only get partial glimpses of the kingdom at any one time.

In order to understand the kingdom, we need some Old Testament background. Old Testament writers make it clear that God is sovereign over all creation, not just the ruler over Israel. But if God is in charge, they thought, why doesn't the world around us reflect God's intention for it? Why are there wars instead of peace, and sickness where God desires healing and wholeness? Why do children go fatherless and the poor remain hungry?

The answer in Scripture is that God will not allow this to go on. God will reorder all things once again to align with God's will for creation and for human beings within that creation. In other words, God will act to restore all things under God's rightful, life-giving authority and rule. God will exercise his reign over creation and the nations once again.

For example, the prophet Isaiah looks forward to the arrival of a messenger who "announces peace, who brings good news, who announces salvation" (52:7 NRSV). Isaiah then summarizes that message as an announcement that God reigns. In other words, all these good things will happen when God restores God's rightful rule. When that happens, the kingdom of God will "come near" (10:9).

What are those good things? Jesus has already named some of them using Isaiah 61:1–2 (Luke 4:18–19): captives will be released, the blind will see, the oppressed and indebted will go free. Jesus is the One who comes to restore God's reign. He heals the sick (14:1–6), he delivers the demon possessed (9:37–43), and he restores the outcasts (17:11–19). God's kingdom will not be here in its fullness until Jesus returns. But it is present in part where God's rule becomes embodied among God's people.

In brief, where God reigns, life is lived as God intended. But for God to reign, for God's kingdom to become present, we must submit ourselves to the one true ruler over all. God does not coerce us. God loves us into placing our lives under God's good care.

1. Honestly taking stock of your life, what aspects of it do you consider as submitted to God and what parts are not?

2. What could you do to bring the whole of your life, as much as you understand it, under God's rule?

WEEK THREE

GATHERING DISCUSSION OUTLINE

A. **Open session in prayer.** Ask that God would astonish us anew with fresh insight from God's Word and transform us into the disciples that Jesus desires for us to become.

B. **View video for this week's readings.**

C. What were the key insights or takeaways that you gained from your reading during the week and from watching the video commentary? In particular, how did these help you to grow in your faith and understanding of Scripture this week? What parts of the Bible lesson or study raised questions for you?

D. **Discuss selected questions from the daily readings.** Invite class members to share key insights or to raise questions that they found to be the most meaningful.

1. **KEY OBSERVATION:** For Jesus, Scripture played a central role in understanding and living into his role in God's mission. God, speaking through Scripture, can do the same for us.

   DISCUSSION QUESTION: Why should God's Word shape our self-understanding?

2. **KEY OBSERVATION:** Jesus' ministry primarily focused on those who had no one else to help them. In doing so, he set the pattern for our own lives as we follow him.

DISCUSSION QUESTION: Among the large numbers of people you encounter on a weekly basis, who would count among the poor? What steps could you take to help them?

3. **KEY OBSERVATION:** Doing life right depends on allowing Jesus to be the ultimate authority in our lives.

   DISCUSSION QUESTION: What would be one practical way you could submit your life to Jesus today?

4. **KEY OBSERVATION:** At its heart, following Jesus necessitates serving others.

   DISCUSSION QUESTION: What one action could you take today that would benefit others rather than yourself?

5. **KEY OBSERVATION:** Life as God intends is found only in submission to God our King.

   DISCUSSION QUESTION: What could you do to bring the whole of your life, as much as you understand it, under God's rule?

E. **As the study concludes, consider specific ways that this week's Bible lesson invites you to grow and calls you to change.** How do this week's scriptures call us to think differently? How do they challenge us to align ourselves with God's work in the world? What specific actions should we take to apply the insights of the lesson into our daily lives? What kind of person does our Bible lesson call us to become?

F. **Close session with prayer.** Emphasize God's ongoing work of transformation in our lives in preparation for loving mission and service in the world. Pray for absent class members as well as for persons whom we need to invite to join our study.

WEEK FOUR

The Sermon on the Plain

ONE

Luke 6:20–26

Luke 6:20–26 *Looking at his disciples, he said: "Blessed are you who are poor, for yours in the kingdom of God. [21]Blessed are you who hunger now, for you will be satisfied. Blessed are you who weep now, for you will laugh. [22]Blessed are you when people hate you, when they exclude you and insult you and reject your name as evil, because of the Son of Man.*

[23]"Rejoice in that day and leap for joy, because great is your reward in heaven. For that is how their ancestors treated the prophets. [24]"But woe to you who are rich, for you have already received your comfort. [25]Woe to you who are well fed now, for you will go hungry. Woe to you who laugh now, for you will mourn and weep. [26]Woe to you when everyone speaks well of you, for that is how their ancestors treated the false prophets."

Key Observation. God's standards of success and failure are not ours.

Understanding the Word. Our text for today begins a distinct section of Jesus' teaching (running through 6:49) known as the "Sermon on the Plain" because Jesus delivered it "on a level place" (6:17). Its content parallels the much longer and better-known "Sermon on the Mount" found in Matthew 5–7.

The immediate background to the sermon is that Jesus had spent all the previous night in prayer. The next morning he selected his twelve disciples (6:12–16). That Jesus would devote such preparation to selecting these individuals indicates the seriousness with which he approached this task. Beginning in verse 20, he instructs a large number of his followers with the

Twelve by his side. What follows forms core teaching for those in the school of Jesus-following.

Jesus used a series of paired, contrasting statements that describe a disciple's basic outlook on life. These paired statements answer fundamental questions: How should we define true success? What heart values should characterize those walking in the path blazed for them by Jesus? As we will see, Jesus laid out a vision that stands in stark contrast to that which his society and ours takes for granted.

Second, these statements pronounce contrasting judgments upon people in different life circumstances. For example, he differentiated the poor (v. 20) from the rich (v. 24), the hungry (v. 21) from the well fed (v. 25). The first of each pairing Jesus pronounced as "blessed" while he declared "woe" to the second, indicating they are not or will not be blessed by God.

Blessedness is not always as it first appears, nor can it be completely exhausted in this life. We naturally tend to think that material riches equate to a blessed life. But the comfort brought about by such abundance can also distort our attitude toward God and those around us. We may come to believe (however subtly) that what we have comes from our own hand and not from God's goodness operating in our lives. As a result, we assume that those without must not be as deserving as we are. But poverty, however difficult, reminds us of our utter dependence on God's provision. As C. S. Lewis famously said in his book *The Problem of Pain*, "God whispers to us in our pleasure . . . but shouts in our pains."*

Hatred can function in the same manner. Insults and rejection from others because of the One we follow keeps us vitally aware of our need of God. But praise from others can lull us into a false sense of security. It is as if we think (again, however subtly), "I guess I do deserve all this."

These verses echo Mary's song of 1:46–55, where God's intention to bless the poor and hungry are first heard. We hear further strands of this teaching when Jesus described his message as "good news" for the poor (4:18). In other words, what Jesus said here is consistent with Luke's message throughout his gospel.

---

*C. S. Lewis, *The Problem of Pain* (New York: Harper Collins, 1940), 93.

1. Think about the people with whom you interact every day at work or in your neighborhood. What standard do you use to evaluate them?
2. How would you treat people differently if you used the standards outlined by Jesus in this passage?

TWO

Luke 6:27–36

Luke 6:27–36 *"But to you who are listening I say: Love your enemies, do good*
to those who hate you, [28]bless those who curse you, pray for those who mistreat
you. [29]If someone slaps you on one cheek, turn to them the other also. If someone
takes your coat, do not withhold your shirt from them. [30]Give to everyone who
asks you, and if anyone takes what belongs to you, do not demand it back. [31]Do
to others as you would have them do to you.

[32]"If you love those who love you, what credit is that to you? Even sinners love
those who love them. [33]And if you do good to those who are good to you, what
credit is that to you? Even sinners do that. [34]And if you lend to those from whom
you expect repayment, what credit is that to you? Even sinners lend to sinners,
expecting to be repaid in full. [35]But love your enemies, do good to them, and lend
to them without expecting to get anything back. Then your reward will be great,
and you will be children of the Most High, because he is kind to the ungrateful
and wicked. [36]Be merciful, just as your Father is merciful.

Key Observation. God calls us to love our enemies.

Understanding the Word. Enemies are easy to find. Does anyone besides me have old friends who cannot stop posting nonsense (meaning positions on which I disagree!) about politics on social media? What about the supervisor who takes credit for your ideas? Or what about that coworker who never carries his or her share of the load with group tasks? Such people become our enemies in the sense that they sap our emotional energy through constant irritation. Even when they are not in our presence, we can find ourselves agitated over something he or she has said. Over time we come to identify ourselves over against them: "I'm glad I'm not jerk like *he* is." If you have someone in your life that fits that description, you've got an enemy.

In the big picture, such enemies are pretty insignificant. After all, as you read this there are people somewhere on planet Earth hiding out for their very lives. Whether their enemies come from another ethnic group, gang, religion, or political movement, their enemies pose genuine danger. Putting up with an aggravating person at work, therefore, pales in comparison. But put up with such folks we must. It is part of life. Count yourself blessed if two or three people you encounter regularly have not popped to mind as you've read this.

Of course, there are two sides to any coin. I am sure that for one reason or another I drive someone nuts. Surely there are people who when they think about me mutter under their breath, "I'm glad I'm not a jerk like *he* is." In other words, we have people we count as our enemies, but we likely fill that role for someone else as well.

In order to live into Jesus' call to love our enemies, we need to keep three truths in mind. First, pop culture has perverted our understanding of love almost beyond recognition by rendering it as something we *feel*. We love someone when *we* feel attracted to them. Nothing could be further from the love of which Jesus speaks here. In biblical terms, love is an active, self-sacrificial pursuit of good for another. Love is not self-referential (how we feel about someone); rather love is *other*-directed. In this sense, love is an *active pursuit* of the good for another.

Second, enacted love toward others includes our response especially when they wrong us. Jesus says, "Do to others as you would have them do to you" (6:31). But this action (as the context makes clear) takes place in response to hateful treatment by others. That's not easy!

Finally, Jesus justifies this call to enemy love by appealing to God's treatment of us: "Be merciful, just as your Father is merciful" (6:36). The apostle Paul states the same thing when he says that when we were God's "enemies" Christ died for us (Rom. 5:10). The standard for determining our treatment of others, even when they wrong us, is not how such actions make us feel; it is how God has treated us—with undeserved mercy.

1. Who would you count as your enemies?
2. What practical actions could you take that would embody Jesus' call to love your enemies?

THREE

Luke 6:37–42

Luke 6:37–42 *"Do not judge, and you will not be judged. Do not condemn,*
and you will not be condemned. Forgive, and you will be forgiven. [38]*Give, and*
it will be given to you. A good measure, pressed down, shaken together and
running over, will be poured into your lap. For with the measure you use, it will
be measured to you."

[39]*He also told them this parable: "Can the blind lead the blind? Will they not*
both fall into a pit? [40]*The student is not above the teacher, but everyone who is*
fully trained will be like their teacher.

[41]*"Why do you look at the speck of sawdust in your brother's eye and pay*
no attention to the plank in your own eye? [42]*How can you say to your brother,*
'Brother, let me take the speck out of your eye,' when you yourself fail to see the
plank in your own eye? You hypocrite, first take the plank out of your eye, and
then you will see clearly to remove the speck from your brother's eye.

Key Observation. We must judge ourselves before judging others.

Understanding the Word. We live within a critical, judgmental society. Social media, whether the latest app on our phone or the news site we visit regularly online, offers a steady stream of negative criticisms of those on the other side of a chosen social or political issue. It isn't just that those with whom we disagree are wrong. They are often portrayed as stupid or morally corrupt. But by characterizing them in this manner, we perform the dangerous move of allowing ourselves not just to overlook our own faults, but to delude ourselves into thinking ours aren't so bad after all!

I find it all too easy to judge others. Let's just say I'm not too patient with the guy looking at his phone in an immobile car in front of me well after the light has turned green. My judgment gets expressed through my car's horn. I think, "What's wrong with that guy? Why doesn't he drive like *I* do?" Or, "Does that woman really need to talk to her children like that? *I'd* never speak to my children in such a nasty manner." In other words, implicit within my fault-finding in others lies the tendency to feed my own ego: "Aren't I wonderful? I'm not like *that*!"

Jesus said that his followers must avoid falling into this all-too-normal pattern of behavior. After all, we walk to the beat of a different drummer. But how do we escape this habit of judging others?

If we are *following* Jesus, the question becomes, How does Jesus view and interact with others when they do wrong in our eyes? After all, Jesus blazed a trail of attitudes, outlooks, and behaviors for us to grow our way into.

Think about how Jesus treated those who would've been easy to judge harshly. He was known for scandalously interacting with "sinners" (see Luke 5:30). He never shied away from those with whom good people found fault. Yes, he called sinners to repentance (along with everyone else). But Jesus saw something in them that other people did not. As a result, he took the time to get to know them.

If we seek out those with whom we disagree, we might find that someone (for example) who sees the results of the last election a bit differently than we do is actually quite a nice person. In other words, if we actually get to know him or her we might find it a bit hard to look down on them.

Jesus' words here should prompt a good look in the mirror. We need to recognize that we are not without fault. We may not drive the way the guy who just cut us off on the highway does, but we still fall short in other ways. If we can gain an honest appraisal of our own shortcomings (see the plank in our own eyes), we'll find judging others much more difficult. And we'll find ourselves much further along the way of Jesus.

1. Among the people with whom you interact on a regular basis, whom do you judge and why do you do so?
2. What practical steps can you take to change your attitudes/actions and take the plank out of your own eye?

FOUR

Luke 6:43–45

Luke 6:43–45 *"No good tree bears bad fruit, nor does a bad tree bear good fruit. [44]Each tree is recognized by its own fruit. People do not pick figs from thornbushes, or grapes from briers. [45]A good man brings good things out of the good* *stored up in his heart, and an evil man brings evil things out of the evil stored up in his heart. For the mouth speaks what the heart is full of.*

Key Observation. Jesus desires good fruit to emerge from our lives.

Understanding the Word. If one thing is true of life in our moment in history it is this: we are bombarded with information. We have televisions in our homes with literally hundreds of channels. Do you think you can avoid television? Think again. Televisions hang from every wall in most restaurants and public buildings. Have to wait in line at the department of motor vehicles? No problem. They've got televisions in the waiting room. Have to wait in the doctor's office? Televisions are there too. Traveling today? No problem. Almost every airport gate has multiple monitors with the ubiquitous CNN blaring non-stop.

Of course, the Internet gives us access to more news and opinions on any selected issue than anyone could possibly absorb. And we can take the Internet with us because we can access it via the phone in our pocket or purse.

Like many of you, I have wondered if all this information really helps us. When I was a youth pastor at the dawn of the digital age, we had our students memorize this saying: "Garbage in. Garbage out." The point was that with all this information within our reach, we had to recognize some important truths.

What we take in *does* shape who we are for good or for ill, whether we like it or not. Do you like the late-night comedians that dominate TV ratings? That's fine. But you have to be aware that large doses of cynicism, however entertaining, breed cynics. Do you enjoy shows about people who overcome steep odds to succeed? If you do, you will likely become an optimist.

We also must be careful what we absorb through media because, well, "Garbage in. Garbage out." Take in what is harmful for us, and what is harmful for others will flow from us. Take in what builds us up, and what encourages others will emerge from our mouths and lives.

Jesus' words here echo a truth found throughout Scripture: who we are emerges from the content of our hearts. The book of Proverbs states it this way, "Above all else, guard your heart, for everything you do flows from it" (4:23). Jesus illustrated this truth by making the useful comparison with fruit trees. An apple tree can only produce apples. That is what apple trees do. If you want oranges, an apple tree cannot help you. Apple trees don't do oranges. We will only produce what is in our hearts.

Our hearts determine what we value and desire above all else. We will know the content of our hearts by what our lives reveal about what we love most. That is the fruit of which Jesus speaks. To what do we devote our time, energy, creativity, and money?

1. In what ways, good or bad, do you see your inner desires and attitudes emerge in your life?
2. What could you change about what you take in that can change what your heart produces in your life?

FIVE

Luke 6:46–49

Luke 6:46–49 NRSV *"Why do you call me 'Lord, Lord,' and do not do what I*
tell you? [47]I will show you what someone is like who comes to me, hears my words,
and acts on them. [48]That one is like a man building a house, who dug deeply
and laid the foundation on rock; when a flood arose, the river burst against that
house but could not shake it, because it had been well built. [49]But the one who
hears and does not act is like a man who built a house on the ground without
a foundation. When the river burst against it, immediately it fell, and great was
the ruin of that house."

Key Observation. We can fully trust our lives to the guidance of Jesus our Lord.

Understanding the Word. When our twins were seventeen years old, they began to dream. A typical conversation sounded like this: "With my job at (fill in the name of a fast food restaurant), I could save enough money by the middle of my senior year to buy a car. Look, here is a BMW for sale on the Internet for only $3,000!" Of course, they also dream that minimum wage job will enable them to travel the world, buy the latest electronic gadgets, and give enough to solve world hunger!

As a result of these dreams, my wife and I spent a good deal of time pushing life advice. "Do you realize that when you buy a car you have only begun to spend money? What about insurance? Do you know there is a reason that BMW costs only $3,000? How much will you need to spend to get it running and to maintain it?"

Our advice is to make a down payment on a car that will serve them well (minimal repairs) until they finish college. Once they graduate and get a real job, then they can save money and buy their second car without going into debt. Our point is this: How can you take steps *now* that will avoid *future* financial problems and enable you to get on your feet financially as you begin adulthood?

After all, we are their parents, and we deeply desire that they live in such a way that they flourish. We have life experience. As a result, we can offer sage advice that will help them. Why would they not follow our counsel?

Jesus' instructions take wise advice about building a life to a whole different level. You build on good foundations or the metaphorical house of your life will be washed away. But note what these foundations consist of: Jesus said, "Why do you call me 'Lord, Lord,' and do not do what I say?" (6:46). Laying an unshakable foundation for life *necessitates* living in obedience to the One we call "Lord." Jesus knows more about us and about our lives than we ever will. Furthermore, Jesus loves us more than we can comprehend. Therefore, Jesus can be trusted with our lives, families, jobs, homes, and concerns. The best way to build our lives on a solid foundation is to live a life of obedience to Jesus.

The fundamental Christian confession is that Jesus is Lord (Rom. 10:9). God has raised Jesus from the dead and seated Jesus at God's right hand as Lord (Eph. 1:20). Recognizing that Jesus is Lord means we submit all we know of ourselves to all we know of God. Why would we entrust ourselves to some other rule in our lives?

1. What do you need to do/not do today in obedience to God?
2. Why would this be wise building?

WEEK FOUR

GATHERING DISCUSSION OUTLINE

A. **Open session in prayer.** Ask that God would astonish us anew with fresh insight from God's Word and transform us into the disciples that Jesus desires for us to become.

B. **View video for this week's readings.**

C. What were the key insights or takeaways that you gained from your reading during the week and from watching the video commentary? In particular, how did these help you to grow in your faith and understanding of Scripture this week? What parts of the Bible lesson or study raised questions for you?

D. **Discuss selected questions from the daily readings.** Invite class members to share key insights or to raise questions that they found to be the most meaningful.

1. **KEY OBSERVATION:** God's standards of success and failure are not ours.

   DISCUSSION QUESTION: How would you treat people differently if you used the standards outlined by Jesus in this passage?

2. **KEY OBSERVATION:** God calls us to love our enemies.

   DISCUSSION QUESTION: What practical actions could you take that would embody Jesus' call to love your enemies?

3. **KEY OBSERVATION:** We must judge ourselves before judging others.

DISCUSSION QUESTION: What practical steps can you take to change your attitudes/actions and take the plank out of your own eye?

4. **KEY OBSERVATION:** Jesus desires good fruit to emerge from our lives.

   DISCUSSION QUESTION: In what ways, good or bad, do you see your inner desires and attitudes emerge in your life?

5. **KEY OBSERVATION:** We can fully trust our lives to the guidance of Jesus our Lord.

   DISCUSSION QUESTION: What do you need to do/not do today in obedience to God?

E. **As the study concludes, consider specific ways that this week's Bible lesson invites you to grow and calls you to change.** How do this week's scriptures call us to think differently? How do they challenge us to align ourselves with God's work in the world? What specific actions should we take to apply the insights of the lesson into our daily lives? What kind of person does our Bible lesson call us to become?

F. **Close session with prayer.** Emphasize God's ongoing work of transformation in our lives in preparation for loving mission and service in the world. Pray for absent class members as well as for persons whom we need to invite to join our study.

WEEK FIVE

Jesus and the Disciples

ONE

Luke 5:1–11 (Part One)

Luke 5:1–11 *One day as Jesus was standing by the Lake of Gennesaret, the
people were crowding around him and listening to the word of God. [2]He saw at
the water's edge two boats, left there by the fishermen, who were washing their
nets. [3]He got into one of the boats, the one belonging to Simon, and asked him to
put out a little from shore. Then he sat down and taught the people from the boat.*

*[4]When he had finished speaking, he said to Simon, "Put out into deep water,
and let down the nets for a catch."*

*[5]Simon answered, "Master, we've worked hard all night and haven't caught
anything. But because you say so, I will let down the nets."*

*[6]When they had done so, they caught such a large number of fish that their
nets began to break. [7]So they signaled their partners in the other boat to come and
help them, and they came and filled both boats so full that they began to sink.*

*[8]When Simon Peter saw this, he fell at Jesus' knees and said, "Go away from
me, Lord; I am a sinful man!" [9]For he and all his companions were astonished
at the catch of fish they had taken, [10]and so were James and John, the sons of
Zebedee, Simon's partners.*

*Then Jesus said to Simon, "Don't be afraid; from now on you will fish for
people." [11]So they pulled their boats up on shore, left everything and followed him.*

Key Observation. Jesus finds followers among people just like us in the midst of our everyday routines.

Understanding the Word. This week we look at Jesus' first encounters with those who would become his key disciples. These first interactions reveal fundamental elements of what it means to follow Jesus. For this reason they demand careful attention.

We tend to read the stories of what Jesus said and did as if they are somehow set apart from normal reality. After all, it's not just every day that the Son of God and Savior of the world stops by the neighborhood! We may be tempted to think there must have been a palpable electricity in the air whenever and wherever Jesus showed up.

But listen to how Luke begins this story, "*One day* as Jesus was standing by the Lake of Gennesaret" (v. 1, emphasis added). Those two simple words, "One day," create a tone of the customary and routine for the utterly non-customary and non-routine events that follow. It's as if Luke wrote, "It could have been any day. It just happened to be this day."

Luke typically portrays Jesus acting within the regular humdrum of daily events. Take this passage for example. At the beginning of Luke 5, a crowd has gathered by a lake to hear him preach. My guess is that they didn't show up at the lake because social media of the day (face-to-face discussions) was alive with the news that Jesus was there. They were at the lakeshore because that was where they spent their lives each and every day. These were people who caught, bought, and sold fish in order to keep a roof over their heads and food on the table. The fact that this well-known teacher showed up at their workplace was the only thing out of the ordinary about this particular day.

We see this same everyday-ness with Peter, James, and John. The smell of the lake, the sound of the birds overhead, and the backs that ache from casting nets into the water and hauling back out again were part of the fabric of their lives. Fishing was what they did. At that point, they were dead tired because they had been out all night fishing (v. 5). Surely their fatigue was intensified because they had no fish to show for their efforts.

But in the midst of a day just like any other, *Jesus interrupted*. Mentally, Peter and his colleagues were already, so to speak, on the drive home. It was time to unplug. But Jesus asked them to cast the nets into the sea one more time, and they did. This was the beginning of their call to follow Jesus. Their lives would never be the same.

We often think Jesus only speaks to really spiritual people (such as a pastor or missionary) and then only in some dramatic setting (such as after a tragic event). But as we see in this text from Luke, Jesus surprises us and meets us as everyday people in the normal events of life.

1. Has God ever gotten your attention out of the blue, in the midst your normal daily activities?
2. How could you look for God to be at work in and through your life today?

TWO

Luke 5:1–11 (Part Two)

Luke 5:1–11 *One day as Jesus was standing by the Lake of Gennesaret, the people were crowding around him and listening to the word of God. [2]He saw at the water's edge two boats, left there by the fishermen, who were washing their nets. [3]He got into one of the boats, the one belonging to Simon, and asked him to put out a little from shore. Then he sat down and taught the people from the boat.*

[4]When he had finished speaking, he said to Simon, "Put out into deep water, and let down the nets for a catch."

[5]Simon answered, "Master, we've worked hard all night and haven't caught anything. But because you say so, I will let down the nets."

[6]When they had done so, they caught such a large number of fish that their nets began to break. [7]So they signaled their partners in the other boat to come and help them, and they came and filled both boats so full that they began to sink.

[8]When Simon Peter saw this, he fell at Jesus' knees and said, "Go away from me, Lord; I am a sinful man!" [9]For he and all his companions were astonished at the catch of fish they had taken, [10]and so were James and John, the sons of Zebedee, Simon's partners.

Then Jesus said to Simon, "Don't be afraid; from now on you will fish for people." [11]So they pulled their boats up on shore, left everything and followed him.

Key Observation. We must decide what we love more than anything else.

Understanding the Word. We live life embedded in communities of various kinds—family, friends, church, school, work, soccer leagues—the list could go on. Within these communities we carry out the business of life. Commitments are made, experiences are shared, and relational bonds are formed as a result.

We only get twenty-four hours in any given day, though. As a result, we all know the tug these commitments and communities place on our time. Should I finish that report for work tonight or go out with friends? Should we go to church on Sunday when our daughter's soccer team holds their first playoff game that morning? Within our busy modern world, the sheer number of communities to which we belong means they compete for our limited time and loyalty. How do we sort through all the demands life places on us?

We are not the first people to deal with these sorts of decisions. In fact, Jesus addressed the issue of competing loyalties head on in his first encounter with his future disciples. In Luke 5:1–11, Jesus used Peter's fishing boat as a platform to address crowds gathered on the shore. He then told these exhausted and fishless fishermen to cast their nets over the side of the boat one more time. Much to their surprise, they caught so many fish that their nets were near the breaking point.

The rightful payoff to these events came when they all returned to shore. Peter, James, and John had experienced enough of Jesus to know what they needed to do next. So, they *left* everything and *followed* Jesus. They faced the issue of competing loyalties: Do we continue with the family business? Or do we commit ourselves to the One who just performed this miracle in our presence?

But what does this all mean for us? After all, Peter may have left the family business of fishing, but I can't just leave my family behind as if they no longer exist. So how do I both leave everything and follow Jesus?

Let's deal with first things first. The core question that must be answered is one of ultimate loyalty: What do we love above all else? Where our first love lies determines the answers to all the other questions in our lives. Therefore we need to settle the ultimate loyalty question first. Then and only then can we sort out other matters.

Yes, we live in a world of competing demands. When all is said and done, what do we value above all else? We may not need to walk away from a job to follow Jesus, but we *do* need to decide upon what we truly love.

Peter, James, and John encountered Jesus. That was enough to decide the question for them. What about you?

1. In all honesty, what does the way you conduct your life say about what you value most?
2. What habits and customs in your life flow from following Jesus above all else?

THREE

Luke 5:27–32 (Part One)

Luke 5:27–32 *After this, Jesus went out and saw a tax collector by the name of Levi sitting at his tax booth. "Follow me," Jesus said to him,* [28]*and Levi got up, left everything and followed him.*

[29]*Then Levi held a great banquet for Jesus at his house, and a large crowd of tax collectors and others were eating with them.* [30]*But the Pharisees and the teachers of the law who belonged to their sect complained to his disciples, "Why do you eat and drink with tax collectors and sinners?"*

[31]*Jesus answered them, "It is not the healthy who need a doctor, but the sick.* [32]*I have not come to call the righteous, but sinners to repentance."*

Key Observation. Repentance consists of turning from one mode of life and pursuing another.

Understanding the Word. The response of Peter, James, and John to Jesus was straightforward. They "left everything and followed him" (5:11). In today's passage Jesus called his next disciple, Levi the tax collector. In doing so, Jesus received the same response: Levi left everything and followed Jesus. We will look at these two episodes together.

This twofold response to Jesus, leaving and following, requires further exploration. The two actions belong together, serving as two sides of the same coin. The disciples turned *from* one manner of life *toward* another. Both activities are necessary. In other words, this process assumes a characteristic orientation and direction to our life. We can turn from one orientation, but our life *will* maintain a direction toward some end. We can't be oriented toward nothing. Turning from requires a turning toward something else.

This twofold action defines what Luke calls *repentance*. A person repents *from* some activity or attitude. Later, Jesus would encounter another tax collector, this one named Zacchaeus (19:1–10). Zacchaeus then turned *from* a life characterized by exploiting people. In doing so, he turned *toward* a life of fairness, generosity, and justice involving those same people (19:8). As a result, Jesus announced that salvation had come to Zacchaeus.

Peter's response to Jesus demonstrated repentance. After Jesus instructed him to cast out his nets one more time and the resulting catch exceeded all expectations, Peter's response seems out of place. Peter told Jesus to leave him alone because he realized, "I am a sinful man" (5:8). But why would this unexpected bountiful catch of fish make Peter realize his sinfulness? Peter apparently realized only God in the person of Jesus could have directed him to such a haul after a long night of fruitless fishing. His only response to the obvious presence and work of God was to recognize his own unworthiness.

In the case of Levi, Luke doesn't tell us much. But we know those who collected taxes on behalf of the Romans were a despised group. They were known for exploiting their power for their own gain. We can see this negative assessment of tax collectors in our passage for today. When Jesus dined with Levi, Pharisees and teachers of the law criticized him for eating with "tax collectors and sinners" (5:30). When Levi left *everything* to follow Jesus, he left behind his lucrative tax business and the ethos that guided it for another manner of life altogether.

Unfortunately, discussions of repentance tend to focus more on what we turn *from* than what we turn *to*. But the former only makes complete sense when we understand the latter. In the case of these first disciples, they redirected their lives to what Luke calls, "following Jesus." Think of the case of Zacchaeus I cited earlier (Luke 19:1–10). He was a chief tax collector. But after encountering Jesus he exclaimed, "if I have cheated anybody out of anything, I will pay back four times the amount" (19:8). He had turned from one manner of life in order to live out another.

1. In concrete terms, what would it look like to turn *from* one pattern in your life that is inconsistent with following Jesus?
2. Today, what is one activity you can do that would be consistent with following Jesus?

FOUR

Luke 5:27–32 (Part Two)

Luke 5:27–32 *After this, Jesus went out and saw a tax collector by the name of Levi sitting at his tax booth. "Follow me," Jesus said to him, [28]and Levi got up, left everything and followed him.*

[29]Then Levi held a great banquet for Jesus at his house, and a large crowd of tax collectors and others were eating with them. [30]But the Pharisees and the teachers of the law who belonged to their sect complained to his disciples, "Why do you eat and drink with tax collectors and sinners?"

[31]Jesus answered them, "It is not the healthy who need a doctor, but the sick. [32]I have not come to call the righteous, but sinners to repentance."

Key Observation. Following Jesus involves purposely associating with social outcasts.

Understanding the Word. Toll collectors (often translated as "tax collectors") were *persona non grata*, people who were not acceptable to or welcomed by others. They were posted along roadways in order to collect tolls on transported goods. These funds paid not only for the local Roman government but were also used by local officials to pay tribute to their Roman overlords in far-away Rome. As such, they were regular reminders to Jews of their imperial subservience.

The problem was not just taxes, but the manner in which they were collected. The Roman government hired local tax collectors to gather a specified amount of money for the Romans. Any funds taken in excess of that amount were kept by the collector himself. Obviously, such an arrangement promoted the worst kinds of abuse and greed. Tax collectors gained a well-earned reputation for charging exorbitant sums in order to line their own pockets. Thus, they became very unwelcome in society.

These details help us make sense of the events in our passage for today. Jesus saw Levi in his tax booth, no doubt while traveling along a road. Levi would have been charged with collecting fees as travelers passed from one section of the country to another. As with Jesus' encounter with Peter, James, and John, Levi left everything behind and followed Jesus. Leaving everything no doubt included not just the practice of collecting taxes, but also the greedy abuse of his power to do so. Levi became associated with Jesus not in some distant or impersonal way, but as a disciple with a teacher. In other words, Jesus claimed among his closest associates one of the most distained people in society.

To add insult to injury (in the eyes of his fellow Jews), Levi hosted a banquet for Jesus in Levi's house. There they dined with other tax collectors and sinners as well. "Sinners" was a term applied to those who violated Jewish law. Eating together in this fashion indicated a level of honor and acceptance extended by Jesus to even *these* people.

All of this points to Jesus' radical acceptance of all who come to him. No one is beyond the reach of God's grace, not even the socially reviled Roman taxmen. But the demand for receiving that grace is simple and total for insiders and outsiders both: follow Jesus alone.

Through his association with social outcasts, Jesus helped define what it means to follow him. Were Jesus to walk through your city or neighborhood, to whom among the *persona non grata* would he choose to reach out with the message of God's love and grace? Would it be the children in foster care? The unemployed? Recent immigrants? What would it take for him to connect with those people? Will you follow him there?

1. Who are the people with whom you find it difficult to associate? Why is that so?
2. In following Jesus, what concrete steps could you take to begin building bridges with these people whom God loves?

FIVE

Luke 5:27–32 (Part Three)

Luke 5:27–32 *After this, Jesus went out and saw a tax collector by the name of Levi sitting at his tax booth. "Follow me," Jesus said to him,* [28]*and Levi got up, left everything and followed him.*

[29]*Then Levi held a great banquet for Jesus at his house, and a large crowd of tax collectors and others were eating with them.* [30]*But the Pharisees and the*

teachers of the law who belonged to their sect complained to his disciples, "Why do you eat and drink with tax collectors and sinners?"

[31]*Jesus answered them, "It is not the healthy who need a doctor, but the sick.*
[32]*I have not come to call the righteous, but sinners to repentance."*

Key Observation. No one is beyond the love and purposes of God.

Understanding the Word. Jesus offended many of his fellow Jews (especially the leaders) by the company he kept. No respectable person dined with such people. And certainly (so they thought) no godly teacher welcomed a tax collector among his followers. But Jesus said the purpose of his ministry involved engaging precisely those whom others rejected.

But think of this engagement from the side of Levi and his fellow tax collectors. Here was this celebrity, the teacher around whom the crowds gathered, the miracle worker who did what only God could do (forgive sins, calm storms). Why in the world would such a holy man be seen with *us*? More than that, why would he join us in a banquet that communicated that he *accepted* us?

I have found such self-doubts about acceptance from God widespread among God's people. In fact, I would say that one of the persistent hindrances to a personal relationship with Jesus is a deep-seated belief that God really cannot love and accept me. God may love other people. God may use other people. But God can't really love, accept, or use me.

The reasons for this vary. But most come back to something like, "You just don't know what I've done." That behavior could have involved a volatile temper, sexual improprieties, indulgence in online pornography, misuse of money, you name it. But the bottom line is the same. God can't really accept me.

But such a belief, however deep-seated and powerful, overlooks the manner in which Jesus engaged people throughout his ministry. No one in first-century Palestine touched lepers with their bare hands. Jesus did and made them socially acceptable ("clean") as a result (5:12–14). Furthermore, Jesus healed the servant of a Roman centurion (7:1–10). Jesus dined with Pharisees, the group often vehemently opposed to him (7:36–50; 14:1–24). He allowed a woman "who lived a sinful life" (likely a prostitute) to anoint his feet with oil (7:37–38), forgiving her sins as the result of this interaction (7:48–50).

Jesus loved and healed the demon-possessed, the blind, and the lame. In all, he welcomed everyone from the complete social outcasts to the community leaders such as the Pharisees. The only people who seem left out are those who owing to pride and self-sufficiency refused to acknowledge their need of God (12:13–21).

A belief that God cannot accept me also denies Jesus' own words about the purpose of his coming. As he stated in our passage for today, "I have not come to call the righteous, but sinners to repentance" (5:32). If you think Jesus came just for those who are acceptable enough, you're missing the point. If you think you've done something too awful for God to welcome you in Christ, you are *the* perfect candidate for welcome into God's kingdom.

As we've seen so far in Luke's gospel, Jesus called for repentance and trust in him. That is, Jesus called for a turning from a claim that, "I can run my own life just fine, thank you" and the life habits that accompany such a claim. That turning from involves turning to a life submitted to Jesus, a life involving a trust-filled following of him.

1. Do you ever think God can accept other people but not you? Why do you think that?
2. Can you now fully trust God to forgive and accept you?

WEEK FIVE

GATHERING DISCUSSION OUTLINE

A. **Open session in prayer.** Ask that God would astonish us anew with fresh insight from God's Word and transform us into the disciples that Jesus desires for us to become.

B. **View video for this week's readings.**

C. What were the key insights or takeaways that you gained from your reading during the week and from watching the video commentary? In particular, how did these help you to grow in your faith and understanding of Scripture this week? What parts of the Bible lesson or study raised questions for you?

D. **Discuss selected questions from the daily readings.** Invite class members to share key insights or to raise questions that they found to be the most meaningful.

1. **KEY OBSERVATION:** Jesus finds followers among people just like us in the midst of our everyday routines.

   DISCUSSION QUESTION: How could you look for God to be at work in and through your life today?

2. **KEY OBSERVATION:** We must decide what we love more than anything else.

   DISCUSSION QUESTION: In all honesty, what does the way you conduct your life say about what you value most?

3. **KEY OBSERVATION:** Repentance consists of turning from one mode of life and pursuing another.

   DISCUSSION QUESTION: Today, what is one activity you can do that would be consistent with following Jesus?

4. **KEY OBSERVATION:** Following Jesus involves purposely associating with social outcasts.

   DISCUSSION QUESTION: Who are the people with whom you find it difficult to associate? Why is that so?

5. **KEY OBSERVATION:** No one is beyond the love and purposes of God.

   DISCUSSION QUESTION: Can you now fully trust God to forgive and accept you?

E. **As the study concludes, consider specific ways that this week's Bible lesson invites you to grow and calls you to change.** How do this week's scriptures call us to think differently? How do they challenge us to align ourselves with God's work in the world? What specific actions should we take to apply the insights of the lesson into our daily lives? What kind of person does our Bible lesson call us to become?

E. **Close session with prayer.** Emphasize God's ongoing work of transformation in our lives in preparation for loving mission and service in the world. Pray for absent class members as well as for persons whom we need to invite to join our study.

WEEK SIX

Prayer

ONE

Luke 5:12–16

Luke 5:12–16 ESV *While he was in one of the cities, there came a man full of leprosy. And when he saw Jesus, he fell on his face and begged him, "Lord, if you will, you can make me clean."* [13]*And Jesus stretched out his hand and touched him, saying, "I will; be clean." And immediately the leprosy left him.* [14]*And he charged him to tell no one, but "go and show yourself to the priest, and make an offering for you cleansing, as Moses commanded, for a proof to them."* [15]*But now even more the report about him went abroad, and great crowds gathered to hear him and to be healed of their infirmities.* [16]*But he would withdraw to desolate places and pray.*

Key Observation. A commitment to undistracted prayer helps keep us in right relationship with God.

Understanding the Word. Prayer formed a central activity of Jesus' life and ministry. Luke devotes greater attention to Jesus' teaching and healing, but he regularly sprinkles his narrative with comments about Jesus praying all night (6:12) or choosing to go into the wilderness to pray (5:16). This week we will look at Jesus' practice of prayer. Even more so we will examine how Jesus taught his disciples to pray. For that teaching contains Jesus' instructions to us as well.

After reporting that Jesus had healed a man with leprosy, Luke informs us that Jesus regularly went to "lonely places" in order to pray. In other words, Jesus could stay among the crowds where his popularity was soaring. He could continue healing and teaching, both vital to his mission. But Jesus chose to go where no one was watching so he could devote himself to prayer.

We learn several truths from Jesus' practice of prayer in this passage. First, Jesus *chose* to pray. Jesus didn't just happen to find himself in "lonely places" as if his GPS told him to take a wrong turn near Lake Gennesaret (5:1). Rather, he determined to go there specifically to pray. Walking there was no easy task. And such a journey may have been dangerous given the presence of thieves along roads in ancient Galilee. Still Jesus determined to do so.

Second, Jesus chose to pray where there would be no distractions. The transition Luke chronicles here is one from Jesus surrounded by great crowds to Jesus surrounded by . . . nothing. When Jesus chose to pray, he chose to pray where he could do so without interruption. It's as if Jesus was trending on social media, then shut off his phone.

Third, Jesus' choice to go away and pray in the midst of effective ministry indicated he knew he needed to pray. Prayer isn't some decoration on top of an otherwise successful ministry. Jesus' ministry of teaching, healing, and restoring required prayer or he would not have made the effort to pray the way he did. Carrying out his call within the mission of God necessitated prayer. Jesus' practice of prayer tells us he knew it to be true.

Fourth, by the construction of his Greek here, Luke tells us this was not a one-off event. This was Jesus' customary *practice*. The ESV rightly captures the sense: Jesus "would withdraw to desolate places and pray" (5:16). The TNIV says, "Jesus often withdrew to lonely places and prayed." Both translations accurately convey Luke's emphasis. Regular, deliberate, undistracted prayer was Jesus' customary way of going about life within God's mission.

Finally, Jesus' prayer life tells us that Jesus was no lone ranger in life and ministry. For all that Jesus did to lead the way within God's purposes, Jesus didn't do what he did on his own. Jesus consciously lived in relation with the Father. Prayer expresses communication within a relationship. Jesus needed time away to hear from and talk to God.

1. Can you identify issues that keep you from praying? Misplaced priorities? Social media? What distracts you?

2. What steps could you take to create undistracted time to pray?

TWO

Luke 11:1–4 (Part One)

Luke 11:1–4 *One day Jesus was praying in a certain place. When he finished, one of his disciples said to him, "Lord, teach us to pray, just as John taught his disciples."* [2]*He said to them, "When you pray, say: 'Father, hallowed be your name, your kingdom come.* [3]*Give us each day our daily bread.* [4]*Forgive us our sins, for we also forgive everyone who sins against us. And lead us not into temptation.'"*

Key Observation. Prayer begins with God, not with us or with our needs.

Understanding the Word. The disciples lived life with Jesus. They walked with him. They ate with him. They certainly laughed with him. They also saw Jesus pray, and they saw him pray regularly. Jesus' life of prayer made such an impression that these disciples/observers were intrigued and challenged. Apparently the same had been true of John the Baptist and his disciples. So Jesus' disciples asked him to teach them to pray.

What resulted was one of the best-known passages in all of Scripture, what we know as the "Lord's Prayer." These words have been recited by God's people for nearly two millennia. That's fine, but I don't think Jesus intended us to simply recite these words as much as he meant for us to use them as a guide for how to pray. Let's look at how he does that in the first phrases of the prayer, "Father, hallowed be your name, your kingdom come."

Before launching into these words, note that Jesus didn't intend for us to pray however we so choose. He instructed his disciples with a specific pattern in mind, "When you pray, say . . ." When we pray as Jesus instructed us to pray, we choose wisely.

"*Father* . . ." Jesus lived his life largely among the sick, the possessed, the outcasts—among those for whom life isn't working. Much of his ministry involved healing and restoring just such people. But notice where he began when he prayed. He didn't begin with needs or with people. Rather he began with God the Father. How unlike the way we normally pray! We're often prompted to pray because of known needs such as sickness or financial problems. Jesus taught us to begin with God.

Jesus was saying that we must first properly orient ourselves toward God before anything else. That happens through a laser-like focus on God alone. Doing so means any needs we have become framed in proper perspective.

"*Hallowed be your name.*" The "name" stands for the person designated by it. In mentioning God's name, Jesus continued his emphasis on the personal, relational element of prayer. But Jesus' point lays in the fact that God deserves to be worshiped. In worshiping God as we pray, we acknowledge God's rule over (and for) all things. In fact, for followers of Jesus, worship is an all-of-life activity. We live all of life in the light of God, God's goodness, and God's mission. God is honored as a result. Prayer simply becomes one more arena of life where we acknowledge God. That may sound intimidating, but worship in word and life is a learned art, a practice and orientation for life into which we grow. Jesus taught us to pray in such a way that enhances that growth.

Worshiping God in prayer also takes our eyes off ourselves. Prayer isn't about us. It's about God, God's goodness, and God's mission. Beginning with worship becomes part of a proper orientation toward God that I mentioned previously.

"*Your kingdom come.*" Life isn't just lived in the presence. By pleading for the kingdom of God to come, we express deep longing for God to end sin and its consequences. In the midst of a world of brokenness, we engage in the mission of God by asking God to make all things right.

1. When you pray, with what concerns do you usually begin?
2. How could you begin a time of prayer today with worship?

THREE

Luke 11:1–4 (Part Two)

Luke 11:1–4 *One day Jesus was praying in a certain place. When he finished, one of his disciples said to him, "Lord, teach us to pray, just as John taught his disciples."* [2]*He said to them, "When you pray, say: 'Father, hallowed be your name, your kingdom come.* [3]*Give us each day our daily bread.* [4]*Forgive us our sins, for we also forgive everyone who sins against us. And lead us not into temptation.'"*

Key Observation. Following Jesus necessitates learning to depend on God for all your needs.

Understanding the Word. With the next phrase of the Lord's Prayer, Jesus maintains a focus on God the Father. At the same time, he begins a transition toward our needs: "*Give us each day our daily bread.*"

With this phrase, Jesus' instructions on prayer center on this trust in God. Life as God intends begins with reverent acknowledgment of God, with placing God above all else (which is what we call "worship"). Consequently, prayer involves asking our Creator and God over all to provide what we need.

At a deep heart level, this may be one of the most genuinely difficult requests to make of God. We live in a world of abundance. For most of us, life just works. We live with a roof over our head. When we turn on the faucet, clean and safe water comes out. When the weather gets hot, we turn on the air conditioning. When the weather gets cold, we turn on the heat. When we get hungry, the refrigerator has food kept fresh. Or we can simply use the app on our phone to get it delivered to our door. For many of us, it's difficult to imagine genuine need.

My wife and I taught at a university in Nairobi, Kenya, for many years. When international television first came into Kenya (in the early 1990s), I recall watching CNN with students. They broke into loud laughter at a story of poor people in Philadelphia. After all, how could a person be poor when (as was the case with the family at the center of the story) they had a roof over their head, a car parked outside, food to eat, and a television in their home? Some in this poor family were obviously overweight. How, a student asked, can a person be poor *and* fat?

In telling this story I don't by any means intend to demean poverty in the United States. Nor do I mean to provoke some guilt trip because of our Western abundance. But my students had witnessed (or experienced) poverty that meant living in a plywood shack with no running water or electricity. In this situation, toilets consisted of communal outhouses down a muddy alley, and baths were taken with water bought by the jug. We simply lack categories to imagine such poverty in the United States.

My point is that we have so much material abundance that it becomes easy to take it for granted. I know I do. Most of us enjoy a standard of life unimaginable for all but the wealthiest few just a century ago.

So how do we learn the dependence on God for which we pray? One way is to practice exceeding generosity. Give financially to kingdom work until it hurts. Once we're stretched, we'll learn how to ask God quickly. The Old Testament says we should give 10 percent of our income to the work of God. That's a good place to begin.

Friends once told us that they begin their giving with 10 percent to their local church (what we usually call a "tithe"). Then they look for additional places to give as needed. That's the right attitude displayed in practice. Like worship, dependence on God is a learned posture toward life. May God help us to be totally dependent on him.

1. What aspects of God's provision in your life do you take for granted?
2. What concrete steps can you take to learn to depend more on God?

FOUR

Luke 11:1–4 (Part Three)

Luke 11:1–4 *One day Jesus was praying in a certain place. When he finished, one of his disciples said to him, "Lord, teach us to pray, just as John taught his disciples."* [2]*He said to them, "When you pray, say: 'Father, hallowed be your name, your kingdom come.* [3]*Give us each day our daily bread.* [4]*Forgive us our sins, for we also forgive everyone who sins against us. And lead us not into temptation.'"*

Key Observation. Jesus invites us to confess our sins and to receive forgiveness.

Understanding the Word. Jesus taught us to ask God for forgiveness. He did so for good reason. One of the fundamental claims of Christianity is that human beings are broken. As a result, we do wrong (or "sin") and need forgiveness.

Paul explains it this way. In Romans 1:21–23 he talks about Adam and Eve and the choices they made regarding how to ultimately orient their lives. Rather than to live in relation to God and who God is, they chose to follow their own desires. As a result, they couldn't understand God's good purposes for them nor could they see life in its proper perspective. As a result, in short, they lived in disobedience to God. They lived "in sin."

Later in Romans 5:12, Paul argues that what Adam began by sinning then spread to all humanity. We all sin because in Adam we are all broken, pulled toward our own desires. To quote an old Frank Sinatra song, each of us wants to live life "my way." In summary, Jesus instructed us to ask God for forgiveness because we need it.

"*Forgive us our sins.*" In this lesson on prayer, Jesus started at the beginning. We ask God for forgiveness. In the terms we talked about previously, asking for forgiveness serves as one part of repentance. We turn *from* sinful actions in part by naming them and asking God to forgive those specific sins.

Learning to pray as Jesus instructed us lays a foundation upon which God can form his character in us. We cannot participate in the abundant life God intends for us if we cling to our own selfish desires and actions. Those longings produce a manner of living that runs counter to a life pleasing to God. By making a request for forgiveness central to our regular communication with God, we seek God's help in conquering precisely those aspects of our life where God's help remains most needed.

We can make Jesus' instructions practical in two ways. First, we can begin by asking God's help to identify those areas where selfishness or fear drives what we do or say. Where does our sinful self interfere in the manner in which we relate to family, neighbors, or coworkers? What are our real goals/desires in life and how do they drive the way we use my money, time, and energy? In other words, a good first step is to ask God for help in identifying where we need forgiveness. As Paul describes it in Romans 1:23, at its core, sin involves deception. We can easily remain unaware of precisely where we need forgiveness.

Second, we ask God for forgiveness and cleansing. Scripture makes clear that God can be trusted to do just that. We don't need to worry that sin gets the last word. First John 1:9 says, "If we confess our sins, he is faithful and just and will forgive us our sins and purify us from all unrighteousness."

1. For what thoughts, actions, or words do you need forgiveness?
2. How can you make prayer for forgiveness a regular part of your life with God?

FIVE

Luke 11:1–4 (Part Four)

Luke 11:1–4 *One day Jesus was praying in a certain place. When he finished, one of his disciples said to him, "Lord, teach us to pray, just as John taught his disciples."* [2]*He said to them, "When you pray, say: 'Father, hallowed be your name, your kingdom come.* [3]*Give us each day our daily bread.* [4]*Forgive us our sins, for we also forgive everyone who sins against us. And lead us not into temptation.'"*

Key Observation. In understanding how God forgives us, we learn to forgive others also.

Understanding the Word. Years ago, friends of ours went through a few difficult years with their teenage son. This wasn't typical teenage rebellion. Rather, the young man passed through a bout of serious depression. The parents had never dealt with depression before so they did not recognize the typical signs of the illness. What they saw and heard was a happy-go-lucky youngster who now vented extreme anger directly at them. He hated them. He wanted them dead. And he expressed those thoughts to them in the most vile language.

I had a long conversation with the father near the end of this ordeal (which turned out positively). He told me that if it wasn't for the profound level at which he understood God's forgiveness of him, he simply could not have forgiven his son. In his words, "If I didn't understand how God refuses to give up on me, I would have given up on my son. But I couldn't ask God to forgive me if I couldn't extend forgiveness to him."

Forgiveness is difficult. We've all experienced the paralyzing pain that comes from being treated wrongly. It happens in any number of ways. It could be a family member who cheats us financially. It may be a coworker or friend who criticizes us behind our backs. The possibilities, as we well know, are endless. But to actually release the resulting pain by forgiving that person is a step that does not come easily.

Learning to practice forgiveness is necessary. We can't live life apart from relationships. Sooner or later some relationships *will* go wrong. To think we can live pain-free is an illusion. The difficult choice to forgive or not to do so will find us in time.

A choice not to forgive eventually leads to bitterness. An African proverb says, "a man who refuses to forgive digs two graves." In other words, we may think we're getting back at some by holding on to our anger, but in reality we're hurting ourselves just as badly or worse.

"*For we also forgive everyone who sins against us.*" Jesus makes clear in his instructions on prayer that our ability to forgive is directly linked to our grasp of God's forgiveness of us. The two go hand in hand. As we saw in the story of my friend, a forgiven person is freed to become a forgiving person. One leads directly to the other.

How do we know whom we need to forgive? Most of us won't find answering that question difficult since we live in target-rich environments. But one way to begin is to ask: Who has hurt me to such an extent that I dwell on that person and that hurt? If we don't forgive that person, we leave them to control our lives. We all know what it means to *dwell* on a past wrong done to us. Left on its own, a refusal to forgive will turn into bitterness. In other words, a refusal to forgive hurts only ourselves.

God can be trusted to forgive us. Once we understand the profound significance of our own sin and God's forgiveness extended to us, then we become freed to extend forgiveness to others.

1. What past wrong done to you do you dwell upon?
2. Can you ask God to help you forgive that person and the hurt they have caused you?

WEEK SIX

GATHERING DISCUSSION OUTLINE

A. **Open session in prayer.** Ask that God would astonish us anew with fresh insight from God's Word and transform us into the disciples that Jesus desires for us to become.

B. **View video for this week's readings.**

C. What were the key insights or takeaways that you gained from your reading during the week and from watching the video commentary? In particular, how did these help you to grow in your faith and understanding of Scripture this week? What parts of the Bible lesson or study raised questions for you?

D. **Discuss selected questions from the daily readings.** Invite class members to share key insights or to raise questions that they found to be the most meaningful.

1. **KEY OBSERVATION:** A commitment to undistracted prayer helps keep us in right relationship with God.

   DISCUSSION QUESTION: What steps could you take to create undistracted time to pray?

2. **KEY OBSERVATION:** Prayer begins with God, not with us or with our needs.

   DISCUSSION QUESTION: How could you begin a time of prayer today with worship?

3. **KEY OBSERVATION:** Following Jesus necessitates learning to depend on God for all your needs.

   DISCUSSION QUESTION: What aspects of God's provision in your life do you take for granted?

4. **KEY OBSERVATION:** Jesus invites us to confess our sins and to receive forgiveness.

   DISCUSSION QUESTION: For what thoughts, actions, or words do you need forgiveness?

5. **KEY OBSERVATION:** In understanding how God forgives us, we learn to forgive others also.

   DISCUSSION QUESTION: What past wrong done to you do you dwell upon?

E. **As the study concludes, consider specific ways that this week's Bible lesson invites you to grow and calls you to change.** How do this week's scriptures call us to think differently? How do they challenge us to align ourselves with God's work in the world? What specific actions should we take to apply the insights of the lesson into our daily lives? What kind of person does our Bible lesson call us to become?

F. **Close session with prayer.** Emphasize God's ongoing work of transformation in our lives in preparation for loving mission and service in the world. Pray for absent class members as well as for persons whom we need to invite to join our study.

WEEK SEVEN

Following Jesus

ONE

Luke 11:27–28

Luke 11:27–28 NRSV *While he was saying this, a woman in the crowd raised her voice and said to him, "Blessed is the womb that bore you and the breasts that nursed you!"* [28]*But he said, "Blessed rather are those who hear the word of God and obey it!"*

Key Observation. We live into God's blessing on our lives when we walk in obedience to God.

Understanding the Word. Jesus taught in order that we might know what following him looks like in real life. This week we continue to explore Jesus' teaching and its implications for how we live day to day.

The caliber of Jesus' teaching and the authority evident in his miracles wowed the gathering crowds (11:14, 27). One woman, amazed at what she had witnessed, pronounced a blessing on Jesus' mother (a culturally appropriate response) for bearing such a son. In doing so, she echoed announcements of blessing on Mary from earlier in Luke (1:42). Seizing the teaching opportunity offered by her blessing, Jesus redefined blessing for his followers.

In biblical terms, being "blessed" means enjoying the favor of God. That favor can take a variety of forms. In the agrarian context of ancient Israel, it could consist of a large number of children and/or livestock. It could also be an apt description of right standing before God no matter one's situation in life. As we saw earlier in Luke (Week Four, Day One), blessedness can be found in being formed into the character of Jesus. In other words, although we tend to think of being blessed as material abundance, in biblical terms that may or may not be the case.

In response to the woman, Jesus did not say she was wrong. But he did offer a mild correction to her understanding of him. The exuberance evident in shouting out her blessing above the noise of the crowd demonstrated her admiration of Jesus. But Jesus said that what really matters, what genuinely produces blessing, was a transformed life of obedience to God's Word.

Luke identifies the *Word* of God with Jesus' teaching. For example, in Luke 5:1 the crowd pressed around Jesus "to hear the word of God" (ESV). The point here is that Jesus didn't just teach so that we might admire his great wisdom. Nor did Jesus speak so that we might have more data for our theological formulations. Rather, Jesus spoke so that we might live into what God is bringing about through his life, death, and resurrection.

Obedience is thus no secondary issue. But it often gets a bad rap. Doing what God asks of us becomes thought of as burdensome. We fear making Christianity simply about compiling a list of dos and don'ts.

But following Jesus through doing what he says enables us to receive God's very best. Through obedience we live into our Creator's design for life. In other words, we place ourselves where we can dwell in God's blessing.

For example, my marriage can only become what God intended when I love my spouse. Friendships can only become the source of profound joy and laughter that God desires when I live a life of integrity and honesty. Work can become meaningful when I carry out my job unto the Lord. Living a life of faithful obedience leads us into the place of God's blessing.

1. In what ways have you seen God's blessing in your life?
2. What one pattern of action could you change so that it becomes more in line with Jesus' teaching?

TWO

Luke 12:13–21

Luke 12:13–21 NRSV *Someone in the crowd said to him, "Teacher, tell my brother to divide the family inheritance with me."* [14]*But he said to him, "Friend,* *who set me to be a judge or arbitrator over you?"* [15]*And he said to them, "Take care! Be on your guard against all kinds of greed; for one's life does not consist in the abundance of possessions."* [16]*Then he told them a parable: "The land of a rich man produced abundantly.* [17]*And he thought to himself, 'What should I do, for I have no place to store my crops?'* [18]*Then he said, 'I will do this: I will pull down my barns and build larger ones, and there I will store all my grain and my goods.* [19]*And I will say to my soul, Soul, you have ample goods laid up for many years; relax, eat, drink, be merry.'* [20]*But God said to him, 'You fool! This very night your life is being demanded of you. And the things you have prepared, whose will they be?'* [21]*So it is with those who store up treasures for themselves but are not rich toward God."*

Key Observation. Do not let your money or possessions define who you are.

Understanding the Word. Funerals typically bring out the worst in families. During breaks in long class sessions, I'll often ask students (most of whom are pastors), "What is the weirdest thing you have seen at a funeral?" The stories range from humorous to utterly tragic. Unfortunately, most of the stories lean toward the latter. Families with no history of conflict suddenly break into open warfare when an inheritance is at stake. According to our passage for today, this tendency for a death to divide families one against another has been going on for a long time.

An anonymous figure in a crowd apparently recognized the depth of Jesus' wisdom on display in his teaching. So, he asked Jesus to settle the family dispute over an inheritance. Jesus refused to answer the man's request directly. Instead, he cut to the heart of the conflict by issuing a warning: "Take care! Be on your guard against all kinds of greed; for one's life does not consist in the abundance of possessions" (12:15).

The problem lay not simply in the conflict between this man and his brother. Rather, the problem stemmed from a false, shared understanding of what's most important in life. They thought the fight was over an inheritance. Jesus said the fight merely forced their greed to come to the surface.

Money in and of itself is neither good nor evil. What matters lies in what we do with it. Better still, what matters lies in what it does with *us*. We use money to feed our family, to clothe ourselves, and to bless others through our giving.

The problem arises when money (and what it can buy) *defines* us. Possessions can make us feel good about ourselves. After all, the BMW (or the pickup truck or whatever) I drive tells everyone "Look at me! I've made it!" We may not say it in so many words, but at a subtle level, we do this. It may not be the vehicle we drive. It could be the house or neighborhood in which we live, where our kids go to school, or the clothes we wear.

Let me tell a story about a couple who kept their possessions in proper perspective. When my wife and I were missionaries, we had to raise every penny of what it took to keep us in Kenya—salary, insurance, travel costs. One generous couple contributed a large portion of our support during our last four years there. Once, when I thanked them for their contributions, they responded, "It's okay, it's not our money anyway. It all belongs to God." That's the proper attitude to have. Own your possessions; don't let them own you.

1. Being totally honest with yourself, what defines you? Wherein lies your value as a human being, parent, child, sibling, coworker, or friend?
2. What steps could you take to make sure your money and/or possessions do not own you?

THREE

Luke 15:11–32

Luke 15:11–32 NRSV *Then Jesus said, "There was a man who had two sons.*
12The younger of them said to his father, 'Father, give me the share of the property
that will belong to me.' So he divided his property between them. 13A few days
later the younger son gathered all he had and traveled to a distant country, and
there he squandered his property in dissolute living. 14When he had spent every-
thing, a severe famine took place throughout that country, and he began to be in
need. 15So he went and hired himself out to one of the citizens of that country,
who sent him to his fields to feed the pigs. 16He would gladly have filled himself
with the pods that the pigs were eating; and no one gave him anything. 17But

when he came to himself he said, 'How many of my father's hired hands have bread enough and to spare, but here I am dying of hunger! [18]I will get up and go to my father, and I will say to him, "Father, I have sinned against heaven and before you; [19]I am no longer worthy to be called your son; treat me like one of your hired hands."' [20]So he set off and went to his father. But while he was still far off, his father saw him and was filled with compassion; he ran and put his arms around him and kissed him. [21]Then the son said to him, 'Father, I have sinned against heaven and before you; I am no longer worthy to be called your son.' [22]But the father said to his slaves, 'Quickly, bring out a robe—the best one—and put it on him; put a ring on his finger and sandals on his feet. [23]And get the fatted calf and kill it, and let us eat and celebrate; [24]for this son of mine was dead and is alive again; he was lost and is found!' And they began to celebrate.

[25]"Now his elder son was in the field; and when he came and approached the house, he heard music and dancing. [26]He called one of the slaves and asked what was going on. [27]He replied, 'Your brother has come, and your father has killed the fatted calf, because he has got him back safe and sound.' [28]Then he became angry and refused to go in. His father came out and began to plead with him. [29]But he answered his father, 'Listen! For all these years I have been working like a slave for you, and I have never disobeyed your command; yet you have never given me even a young goat so that I might celebrate with my friends. [30]But when this son of yours came back, who has devoured your property with prostitutes, you killed the fatted calf for him!' [31]Then the father said to him, 'Son, you are always with me, and all that is mine is yours. [32]But we had to celebrate and rejoice, because this brother of yours was dead and has come to life; he was lost and has been found.'"

Key Observation. Take joy in the good things that happen to others.

Understanding the Text. The parable of the prodigal son stands as one of the most cherished stories in all of the Bible. It is not hard to understand why since we recognize ourselves in one or more of the parable's characters.

We are familiar with the parable's story line. The younger of two sons asks his father for his inheritance while the father is still alive. The father concedes. But rather than use this windfall wisely, the son flees from his family and parties away the entirety of the money. He finds himself hungry, penniless, and alone. He has become a prodigal from his own home and family.

The story invites us to imagine his guilt and shame. He has disappointed those closest to him. In a culture where family honor was paramount, he has brought shame upon his own father. And it is all on him. He alone has let them down. And now he is out of options.

That's when the story takes its first surprise turn. The son goes back to his father and the family he himself spurned. He returns with nothing but the disgrace and guilt he so foolishly brought upon them all. But it's what happens when he returns that anchors this parable's place in our memory. At best, we expect the son to receive the rebuke he so well deserves. We wonder if the father will even take him back at all. Contrary to expectations, the father welcomes him back with open arms, even honoring the son with a feast.

We have rightly understood this parable as a reflection of God's undeserved love lavished on us. In the prodigal son, we recognize our own waywardness, even if we haven't gone to the lengths of the younger son in our own sin. We also see ourselves as recipients of God's unexpected and undeserved love just like the son receives from his father.

We often stop reading the parable at that point. After all, who doesn't love a great ending? But the parable continues and Jesus' primary point lies in the final paragraph. The elder son, the one who did not rebel and bring shame upon his family, returns from working in the fields to find everyone celebrating his brother's return. At this point the parable takes a second unexpected turn.

The older son becomes angry over the celebration of his brother's return. The older son had remained faithful to his father. Yet his father never rewarded him with a party. The father affirms his love for the older son. But he also reminds him that his younger brother had been given up for dead. Now that he has surprisingly returned, shouldn't they all celebrate together?

Like the older brother, we easily feel we are more deserving. As a result, we can find it difficult to rejoice when good things happen to a colleague at work or to a neighbor. But God calls us to rejoice with those who rejoice for *their* sake, not for ours.

1. Have you ever felt cheated when someone else was rewarded and you were not?
2. With whom can you rejoice today?

FOUR
Luke 9:46–48

Luke 9:46–48 NRSV *An argument arose among them as to which one of them was the greatest. [47]But Jesus, aware of their inner thoughts, took a little child and put it by his side, [48]and said to them, "Whoever welcomes this child in my name welcomes me, and whoever welcomes me welcomes the one who sent me; for the least among all of you is the greatest."*

Key Observation. In God's kingdom, greatness is defined by serving others.

Understanding the Text. We debate about who or what is the greatest. This is especially true when it comes to sports. Lebron James or Michael Jordan? Christiano Ronaldo or Lionel Messi? We get bombarded with additional greatest questions at the end of every year: What was the best movie? What were the five best books? My children even playfully taunt one another over who was their grandmother's favorite grandchild. We love such questions because *we like to argue about who or what is the greatest.*

But debates over who is the greatest can get personal and painful. We know how this happens. People at work compete with (and against) each other to see who gets that promotion. Among children and teenagers, the tensions arise over who is whose best friend. We recognize that so much of this competition is nothing but pettiness. But we take part in it anyway!

It may come as a surprise then to find Jesus' own disciples argued over who was greatest *among them*. Why would these folks, Jesus' closest followers of all people, fight over such an issue?

Here is what was happening. Peter, likely speaking for the others as well, recognized that Jesus was "God's Messiah" (9:20). The Messiah was understood to be a coming king from the line of David who would deliver and restore Israel. As we see, that's precisely who Jesus is.

But the disciples misunderstood what Jesus' kingship is all about. They thought Jesus would be a king just like any other king. That means he would wield earthly power in a manner just like any other king as well. And if Jesus was going to sit on a throne in Jerusalem and rule over Israel, he would need honored officials to sit on his right and left hand. They also would wield power as the king's immediate subordinates. In other words, the disciples were arguing over who got to sit in these seats of earthly power, honor, and status.

Jesus said his kingdom isn't like that. With Jesus, greatness wouldn't be defined by who makes it to the hall of fame, who draws the largest salary, or who exerts power over others. Rather, serving others defines greatness. Jesus himself would model this ethic of service by voluntarily going to die for the sins of others. An ethic of service would define Jesus' followers as well. In sum, against all appearances, those whom we don't notice but who embody a life of service will count as worthy of honor and status.

1. What do you think counts for greatness in life?
2. What practical steps could you take to follow in Jesus' footsteps and serve others?

DAY FIVE

Luke 17:11–19

Luke 17:11–19 NRSV *On the way to Jerusalem Jesus was going through the region between Samaria and Galilee.*
[12]As he entered a village, ten lepers approached him. Keeping their distance,
[13]they called out, saying, "Jesus, Master, have mercy on us!"
[14]When he saw them, he said to them, "Go and show yourselves to the priests." And as they went, they were made clean.
[15]Then one of them, when he saw that he was healed, turned back, praising God with a loud voice.
[16]He prostrated himself at Jesus' feet and thanked him. And he was a Samaritan.
[17]Then Jesus asked, "Were not ten made clean? But the other nine, where are they?
[18]Was none of them found to return and give praise to God except this foreigner?"
[19]Then he said to him, "Get up and go on your way; your faith has made you well."

Key Observation. Make giving thanks to God and to other people a daily practice.

Understanding the Word. Ten lepers approached Jesus. Well aware of their despised social status, they kept their distance. In fact, they stayed far enough away that they have to call out to Jesus to get his attention. Luke tells us little about their encounter other than that they asked Jesus to extend mercy to them—apparently, a plea to alleviate their extreme misery. Jesus did nothing but told them to show themselves to the priests (who could judge whether or not someone was clean). When the lepers left to fulfill Jesus' instructions, Luke tells us "they were made clean." In other words, they were healed.

The miraculous healing of the ten lepers isn't the point of Luke's story, though. Nine of the ten simply disappear from the narrative. One former leper, however, realizes who was responsible for his cleansing. He alone returned to Jesus, praising God and thanking Jesus. For Jesus had done the utterly unimaginable for him. But Jesus noted the obvious question that remained. Where were the other nine? Only one came back to say thanks?

Gratitude is such a simple matter. None of us will likely experience such a dramatic transformation as the lepers did. But we all have reason to thank God or another person for the good things in our lives. Few actions we can take can prove so transformative for us and for others.

Here are a couple of examples from my own life. A few weeks ago, my oldest son texted to thank me for taking him to a skateboard park twenty years ago. As an early teen, skateboarding was his passion. Skateboard parks with half pipes and rails were a new thing at the time and so there were few of them. But we had heard of a new park opening not far from where we lived. One day without telling him where we were going, my wife and I bundled him into the car. He was stunned when he saw the skate park. For him it was a dream come true. And he skated until he was ready to drop. Over the years, my wife and I had forgotten about that outing. It really wasn't that big a deal for us. But he didn't. And twenty years later, he remembered to say thanks.

Here's another. I do a good bit of writing in a local coffee shop/bakery. I see the bakery as a gift to our community. The regulars gather regularly. Conversations blossom. And I have a wonderful place for dates with my wife and with my daughters. I've made it a practice to tell the owner, Angie, and the staff how much I appreciate what they do. Angie's workday begins around 2:00 a.m. The croissants alone take eighteen hours to prepare. But so many benefit from her labor of love. So I thank her regularly.

Saying thank you is so simple, whether it be to God or to the people God brings across our path. What a wonderful practice it would be to make it part of our daily life!

1. To whom can you say thank you today?
2. How could you make thanking God and thanking people a regular part of your life as you follow Jesus?

WEEK SEVEN

GATHERING DISCUSSION OUTLINE

A. **Open session in prayer.** Ask that God would astonish us anew with fresh insight from God's Word and transform us into the disciples that Jesus desires for us to become.

B. **View video for this week's readings.**

C. What were the key insights or takeaways that you gained from your reading during the week and from watching the video commentary? In particular, how did these help you to grow in your faith and understanding of Scripture this week? What parts of the Bible lesson or study raised questions for you?

D. **Discuss selected questions from the daily readings.** Invite class members to share key insights or to raise questions that they found to be the most meaningful.

1. **KEY OBSERVATION:** We live into God's blessing on our lives when we walk in obedience to God.

   DISCUSSION QUESTION: What one pattern of action could you change so that it becomes more in line with Jesus' teaching?

2. **KEY OBSERVATION:** Do not let your money or possessions define who you are.

   DISCUSSION QUESTION: Being totally honest with yourself, what defines you? Wherein lies your value as a human being, parent, child, sibling, coworker, or friend?

3. **KEY OBSERVATION:** Take joy in the good things that happen to others.

   DISCUSSION QUESTION: With whom can you rejoice today?

4. **KEY OBSERVATION:** In God's kingdom, greatness is defined by serving others.

   DISCUSSION QUESTION: What practical steps could you take to follow in Jesus' footsteps and serve others?

5. **KEY OBSERVATION:** Make giving thanks to God and to other people a daily practice.

   DISCUSSION QUESTION: To whom can you say thank you today?

E. **As the study concludes, consider specific ways that this week's Bible lesson invites you to grow and calls you to change.** How do this week's scriptures call us to think differently? How do they challenge us to align ourselves with God's work in the world? What specific actions should we take to apply the insights of the lesson into our daily lives? What kind of person does our Bible lesson call us to become?

F. **Close session with prayer.** Emphasize God's ongoing work of transformation in our lives in preparation for loving mission and service in the world. Pray for absent class members as well as for persons whom we need to invite to join our study.

WEEK EIGHT

Jesus in Jerusalem

ONE

Luke 19:28–40

Luke 19:28–40 ESV *And when he had said these things, he went on ahead, going up to Jerusalem.* [29]*When he drew near to Bethphage and Bethany, at the mount that is called Olivet, he sent two of the disciples,* [30]*saying, "Go into the village in front of you, where on entering you will find a colt tied, on which no one has ever yet sat. Untie it and bring it here.* [31]*If anyone asks you, 'Why are you untying it?' you shall say this: 'The Lord has need of it.'"* [32]*So those who were sent went away and found it just as he had told them.* [33]*And as they were untying the colt, its owners said to them, "Why are you untying the colt?"* [34]*And they said, "The Lord has need of it."* [35]*And they brought it to Jesus, and throwing their cloaks on the colt, they set Jesus on it.* [36]*And as he rode along, they spread their cloaks on the road.* [37]*As he was drawing near—already on the way down the Mount of Olives—the whole multitude of his disciples began to rejoice and praise God with a loud voice for all the mighty works that they had seen,* [38]*saying, "Blessed is the King who comes in the name of the Lord! Peace in heaven and glory in the highest!"* [39]*And some of the Pharisees in the crowd said to him, "Teacher, rebuke your disciples."* [40]*He answered, "I tell you, if these were silent, the very stones would cry out."*

Key Observation. Jesus deserves our worship.

Understanding the Word. After a period of ministry in Galilee (4:14–9:50 ESV), Luke reports that Jesus "set his face to go to Jerusalem" (9:51 ESV). Jerusalem played an important role in Jesus' story. Earlier Jesus was presented to God in the temple in Jerusalem (2:22). Then he returned there. There the gospel reaches its climax with Jesus' death and resurrection (23:44–24:12). This week we begin with Jesus' entry into the city (19:28–40). We will continue by examining critical events that happened there.

Three events marked Jesus' entry into Jerusalem. First, he sent two of his disciples ahead of him with detailed instructions for finding a colt on which he could enter the city (in fulfillment of Zechariah 9:9). What Jesus said would happen when they found the colt took place just as Jesus said it would. Jesus' knowledge of how things would take place indicated he would not just be a passive victim of what was about to take place. He knew what would happen and moved ahead willingly.

Second, when Jesus rode into the city, an apparently large crowd of disciples rejoiced. They praised God with a "loud voice" (19:37 ESV) because of all they had seen Jesus do. The first part of their acclamation of Jesus came from Psalm 118:26, "Blessed is he who comes in the name of the LORD!" (19:38). In ancient Israel, this psalm was sung to honor a newly crowned king. So the crowds welcomed Jesus to Jerusalem as king (keep in mind that the *Messiah* was a royal figure). The second part echoed the song of the heavenly chorus sung at Jesus' birth, "Glory to God in the highest, and on earth peace among those with whom he is pleased!" (2:14 ESV). This fact gives the scene an ironic twist. Although the crowds welcomed Jesus as their king, we know this king had come to Jerusalem in order to be put to death.

Finally, some Pharisees who witnessed these events told Jesus to rebuke his disciples. After all, declaring someone to be the *king* of the Jews could have gotten them in trouble with their Roman overlords. In fact, at Jesus' trial and during his crucifixion, Jesus would be mocked for claiming to be "King of the Jews." It's as if the Romans said, "*This* is what happens to anyone claiming to be king when we rule over you!" Actually, Jesus really is Israel's king. The Romans just didn't know it. Jesus' response to the Pharisees was telling, "if these [people] were silent, the very stones would cry out" (19:40 ESV). He could not stop the truth from becoming known.

Thus, the crowds acclaimed Jesus as Israel's king. But in doing so, they *worshiped* Jesus. Such worship cannot be stopped. These were the people who had witnessed Jesus forgive sins (5:20–26). Only God forgives sin. Jesus had demonstrated command over natural forces (8:22–25). Only God does that.

The proper response to King Jesus as he entered Jerusalem was worship. If the crowd of disciples ceased to do so, Jesus said, even the stones would acknowledge the truth.

1. Why do you think Jesus deserves your worship?
2. How can you worship Jesus with your words, deeds, and attitudes?

TWO

Luke 20:45–21:4

Luke 20:45–21:4 ESV *And in the hearing of all the people he said to his disciples, 46"Beware of the scribes, who like to walk around in long robes, and love greetings in the marketplaces and the best seats in the synagogues and the places of honor at feasts, 47who devour widows' houses and for a pretense make long prayers. They will receive the greater condemnation."*

21:1Jesus looked up and saw the rich putting their gifts into the offering box, 2and he saw a poor widow put in two small copper coins. 3And he said, "Truly, I tell you, this poor widow has put in more than all of them. 4For they all contributed out of their abundance, but she out of her poverty put in all she had to live on."

Key Observation. Place your trust in God, not in money and status.

Understanding the Word. I have heard it said that Jesus talked about no other subject more often than money. That may be true. I haven't counted up the verses myself. But money certainly played an important role in Jesus' teaching overall. And that's for good reason. Perhaps nothing in life reveals where our heart truly lies more than what we do with our money.

Jesus had some harsh words on the subject. "Woe to you who are rich" (6:24 ESV). "You cannot serve God and money" (16:13 ESV). At the same time, he didn't condemn everything having to do with money. Luke records that some apparently wealthy women supported Jesus and his disciples (8:2–3). Jesus also commended a woman who anointed him with costly oil (7:36–50).

So money in and of itself is morally neutral. But Jesus didn't mince words. Money poses a potentially great risk to our relationship with God.

The events in today's text took place in the Jerusalem temple. We tend to think of the temple in purely religious terms. After all, the temple was the place where sacrifices were made to God. But the temple served as the social, political, and economic center for Jews as well. The temple maintained a treasury within its precincts. Gifts contributed to its coffers were then used to support the poor.

The incident involving this poor widow falls within a series of episodes where Jesus criticized practices of giving in the temple. Apparently, the educated elite and wealthy leaders liked to appear in the temple area. Doing so offered an opportunity for affirmation of their social standing and honor. So they walked around in long robes and relished being greeted by others. The greetings served as social recognition of just how important they really were. In other words, walking through the temple area and contributing to its treasury was about *them*.

Money creates opportunities. With it we can buy stuff—vacations, particular kinds of cars, fashionable clothes. Just watch advertising on television. You'll see all the things money can buy that will make you *someone* in the eyes of others. We can become like those walking about in fine robes, awaiting our recognition from those around us.

From the outset of Luke's gospel, we've been told that Jesus would reverse signs of status and honor. Mary exclaims,

> He [God] has shown the strength with his arm;
>   he has scattered the proud in the thoughts of their hearts;
> he has brought down the mighty from their thrones
>   and exalted those of humble estate;
> he has filled the hungry with good things,
>   and the rich he has sent away empty (1:51–53 ESV)

In our text for today, we see this program played out. Those that used their wealth and status as means to prop up their identity and importance received Jesus' rebuke. In contrast, the poor widow used what she had with pure motives. She gave generously out of trust in God, not to draw attention to herself.

1. Be honest. What do you believe ultimately determines how you think others think of you?
2. What would a God-trusting, God-centered identity look like?

THREE

Luke 22:1–6, 47–48

Luke 22:1–6, 47–48 ESV *Now the Feast of Unleavened Bread drew near, which is called the Passover. [2]And the chief priests and the scribes were seeking how to put him to death, for they feared the people.*

[3]The Satan entered into Judas called Iscariot, who was of the number of the twelve. [4]He went away and conferred with the chief priests and officers how he might betray him to them. [5]And they were glad, and agreed to give him money. [6]So he consented and sought an opportunity to betray him to them in the absence of a crowd. . . .

[47]While he was still speaking, there came a crowd, and the man called Judas, one of the twelve, was leading them. He drew near to Jesus to kiss him, [48]but Jesus said to him, "Judas, would you betray the Son of Man with a kiss?"

Key Observation. Keep your eyes on God, not on human leaders.

Understanding the Word. The story of Jesus comes filled with unexpected developments. His disciples who walked with him daily often failed to understand him (9:45). The Jewish leaders who you would expect to recognize Israel's own Messiah did not (5:21). Jesus commended a manager who acted, so it appears, unjustly (16:1–13).

But nothing catches us off guard more than the fact that one of those closest to Jesus betrayed him. How could someone who spent that much time listening to *the* Teacher teach turn on him? Why would a follower who had watched the power of God operate through Jesus to heal the sick and to deliver the possessed prove so disloyal? I mean, Judas was on the career path toward the Jesus-following hall of fame! How could he do *this*?

What do we learn from the fact that Jesus was betrayed by one in whom he had invested so much? After all, Judas may have been the first follower of Jesus to fail. But we all know he wasn't the last.

The fall of visible Christian leaders has been all too common through Christian history. In recent times, such failures seem rife among TV preachers or leaders of high-profile churches. Typically, the sins are sexual—the leader has an affair with a staff member or congregant. At times, the problems stem from misuse of money.

The aftermath of the sins of visible Christian leaders is devastating. Churches split apart. The larger public scoffs at Christians who preach one thing while doing another. And some individuals stop following Jesus altogether.

We have had personal experience with leadership failure. A few years ago, the teaching pastor at our church abruptly resigned. It turned out he had been having an affair with his secretary. Christians across the city were stunned. This young man in his mid-thirties was a gifted communicator. He was widely recognized as a rising Christian leader among his generation. A year later, in deep depression, he took his own life.

What happened as a result? Some people did leave the church. But among those who remained, we often heard a story that went something like this, "He always taught us *not* to look to him or to any other human being, but to God. If we follow what he taught us, our faith won't depend on the example of any one gifted individual, not even him."

Therein lies the key. We keep our eyes on Jesus. Our faith does not rest in any human leader however gifted he or she might be.

God does raise up leaders among us. They model what a genuine following of Jesus looks like. They teach truth and lead us in worship. We should honor them for their service. But they are human beings just like us. Remember, true Christian leaders point us to Jesus, not to themselves.

1. Do you know a Christian leader who has failed morally?
2. How can you keep your eyes on Jesus rather than on leaders God raises up among us?

FOUR

Luke 23:32–43

Luke 23:32–43 ESV *Two others, who were criminals, were led away to be put
to death with him.* 33*And when they came to the place that is called The Skull,
there they crucified him, and the criminals, one on his right and one on his left.*
34*And Jesus said, "Father, forgive them, for they know not what they do." And
they cast lots to divide his garments.* 35*And the people stood by, watching, but
the rulers scoffed at him, saying, "He saved others; let him save himself, if he is
the Christ of God, his Chosen One!"* 36*The soldiers also mocked him, coming up
and offering him sour wine* 37*and saying, "If you are the King of the Jews, save
yourself!"* 38*There was also an inscription over him, "This is the King of the Jews."*

39*One of the criminals who were hanged railed at him, saying, "Are you not
the Christ? Save yourself and us!"* 40*But the other rebuked him, saying, "Do you
not fear God, since you are under the same sentence of condemnation?* 41*And we
indeed justly, for we are receiving the due reward of our deeds; but this man has
done nothing wrong."* 42*And he said, "Jesus, remember me when you come into
your kingdom."* 43*And he said to him, "Truly, I say to you, today you will be with
me in paradise."*

Key Observation. It's never too late to turn to God.

Understanding the Word. I wish I were perfect. But I'm not. Ask my wife and kids if you don't believe me! Like all human beings I come flawed in ways large and small. The apostle Paul states this truth as follows, "for all have sinned and fall short of the glory of God" (Rom. 3:23). Life exempts no human being from sin's impact. It mars us all.

For this reason, human repentance serves as the necessary requirement for entering into a relationship with God. We have to turn from our selfish manner of life to follow Jesus. To put it another way, we cannot clean up our act sufficiently to become acceptable to God on our own. If we're human, we won't be perfect.

Today's passage contains one of the most memorable episodes in the story of Jesus' crucifixion. Jesus had been viciously beaten and mocked by Roman soldiers. Ironically, the soldiers mocked Jesus by calling him "King of the Jews" and "the Christ of God, his Chosen One!" Against all appearances, that is precisely who he is. Jesus demonstrated his kingship by dying on behalf of others.

In the midst of this chaotic scene, we learn two other people had been crucified alongside Jesus. Luke names neither man; nor are we told the specific nature of their crime. We are only told they were criminals. One man joined in with the mockers of Jesus. He shouted to Jesus, "Are you not the Christ? Save yourself and us!" In response, the other criminal rebuked the first. He acknowledged that they each deserved their punishment. But Jesus is innocent. He then turned to Jesus and requested, "Jesus, remember me when you come into your kingdom" (v. 42).

The second criminal, on a cross next to Jesus of all places, recognized the truth of who Jesus is. As part of that recognition, we hear overtones of repentance in his request for Jesus to remember him. At that late moment, after hours of torture at the hands of the Roman soldiers, this man recognized the true King in the defining act of his kingship.

Jesus' response grabs our attention. He acknowledged the man's faith, "Truly, I say to you, today you will be with me in paradise." Jesus freely welcomed a crucified criminal as one of his own.

The remarkable truth on display in this episode lay in Jesus' willingness to accept even a crucified man. Crucifixion not only inflicted unimaginable pain. According to ancient sources, nothing was more degrading and humiliating than to be fixed to a cross to die. But as with other outcasts, Jesus didn't hesitate. Even crucified criminals who turn to him found welcome.

The point of this passage is that it's never too late to turn to God. Nothing will stay in your way. If God could accept a criminal on the cross, God can readily accept us whatever our imperfections or wrongdoing.

1. Do you ever doubt God loves and accepts you? Why is that so?
2. What is one area of your life that you can totally commit to God today?

FIVE

Luke 24:36–49

Luke 24:36–49 ESV *As they were talking about these things, Jesus himself stood among them, and said to them, "Peace to you!"* [37]*But they were startled and frightened and thought they saw a spirit.* [38]*And he said to them, "Why are you troubled, and why do doubts arise in your hearts?* [39]*See my hands and my feet, that it is I myself. Touch me, and see. For a spirit does not have flesh and bones as you see that I have."* [40]*And when he had said this, he showed them his hands and his feet.* [41]*And while they still disbelieved for joy and were marveling, he said to them, "Have you anything here to eat?"* [42]*They gave him a piece of broiled fish,* [43]*and he took it and ate before them.*

[44]*Then he said to them, "These are my words that I spoke to you while I was still with you, that everything written about me in the Law of Moses and the Prophets and the Psalms must be fulfilled."* [45]*Then he opened their minds to understand the Scriptures,* [46]*and said to them, "Thus it is written, that the Christ should suffer and on the third day rise from the dead,* [47]*and that repentance for the forgiveness of sins should be proclaimed in his name to all nations, beginning from Jerusalem.* [48]*You are witnesses of these things.* [49]*And behold, I am sending the promise of my Father upon you. But stay in the city until you are clothed with power from on high."*

Key Observation. God calls and empowers us to tell others about Jesus.

Understanding the Word. This passage draws the gospel of Luke to a close and begins the transition to Luke's second volume, the Acts of the Apostles. It begins with the disciples gathered around a fire eating fish. Once a fisherman, always a fisherman, I guess. At this point Jesus appeared among them in order to verify that God had indeed raised him from the dead. He had real flesh and bones. He got hungry, and he ate fish. In other words, he was not some disembodied spirit. This was the same Jesus they walked with for years.

What were the disciples to make of all this? They knew Jesus. They walked with him for what was likely about three years. They laughed with him. They heard him argue with Jewish leaders. They listened to him teach and saw him perform miracles. But they also knew he was brutally put to death by the Romans. And now he's *alive*? How could this be?

Jesus reassured them. According to the Old Testament, his death and resurrection had been part of God's plan all along. And God's plan *was* coming to fruition. Jesus really is alive!

The message of repentance and forgiveness must be proclaimed to all nations. This good news could not be kept to themselves or to their fellow Jews. God intended its impact to resound to all the peoples of the world.

And God had chosen them to be the first proclaimers of this message. They saw what God had done through Jesus from the beginning until the present. They knew it better than anyone else. They must give *witness* to the nations of what God had done.

Jesus placed one qualification on them. The disciples must wait until Jesus poured out the Holy Spirit on them. Only then could they do what God had appointed them to do. After all, getting the good news to the nations would be God's business. The disciples had been invited to take part in what God was doing. The Holy Spirit would empower them to get it done.

All of these developments in the plan of God hinged on the fact that God raised Jesus from the dead. If Jesus remained in the grave for his body to rot away like any other human that would prove he had been a great teacher and nothing more. His claim to be the Son of God would have been mistaken. The work of God would have ceased at that point. Paul says it this way, "if Christ has not been raised, your faith is futile and you are still in your sins" (1 Cor. 15:17 ESV).

But God did in fact raise him from the dead. In the next stage of this story (Acts 1), Jesus would return to God's right hand where he would reign as Lord. From there he would pour out his Holy Spirit on the disciples and the next stage of God's mission to the nations would begin.

1. Has God done anything in your life that you can tell others about?
2. Can you ask God to empower you to do so?

WEEK EIGHT

GATHERING DISCUSSION OUTLINE

A. **Open session in prayer.** Ask that God would astonish us anew with fresh insight from God's Word and transform us into the disciples that Jesus desires for us to become.

B. **View video for this week's readings.**

C. What were the key insights or takeaways that you gained from your reading during the week and from watching the video commentary? In particular, how did these help you to grow in your faith and understanding of Scripture this week? What parts of the Bible lesson or study raised questions for you?

D. **Discuss selected questions from the daily readings.** Invite class members to share key insights or to raise questions that they found to be the most meaningful.

1. **KEY OBSERVATION:** Jesus deserves our worship.

   DISCUSSION QUESTION: How can you worship Jesus with your words, deeds, and attitudes?

2. **KEY OBSERVATION:** Place your trust in God, not in money and status.

   DISCUSSION QUESTION: Be honest. What do you believe ultimately determines how you think others think of you?

3. **KEY OBSERVATION:** Keep your eyes on God, not on human leaders.

DISCUSSION QUESTION: How can you keep your eyes on Jesus rather than on leaders God raises up among us?

4. **KEY OBSERVATION:** It's never too late to turn to God.

   DISCUSSION QUESTION: What is one area of your life that you can totally commit to God today?

5. **KEY OBSERVATION:** God calls and empowers us to tell others about Jesus.

   DISCUSSION QUESTION: Has God done anything in your life that you can tell others about?

F. Close session in prayer.

www.ingramcontent.com/pod-product-compliance
Ingram Content Group UK Ltd.
Pitfield, Milton Keynes, MK11 3LW, UK
UKHW021401070726
13610UKWH00012B/69

9 781628 246810